#COMPLETELYMARRIED

Journey to the Altar and Beyond

Damien K. H. Nash
and
Kenady Nash

Also by Damien K. H. Nash

#CompletelySingle
How to Load Your Truck
Thoughts From the Box

Gift Presented

To:

_____

From:

_____

Date:

DAMIEN K. H. NASH AND KENADY NASH

#COMPLETELYMARRIED

#COMPLETELYMARRIED

Journey to the Altar and Beyond

Damien K. H. Nash
and
Kenady Nash

#CompletelyMarried: Journey to the Altar and Beyond
© 2020 Damien K. H. Nash and Kenady Nash
All rights reserved.

No part of this publication may be reproduced, distributed, or transmitted in any form or by any means, including photocopying, recording, or other electronic or mechanical methods, without the prior written permission from the publisher, except in the case of brief quotations embodied in critical reviews and certain other noncommercial uses permitted by copyright law. For permission requests, write to the publisher.

Scripture quotations marked (BSB) are taken from The Holy Bible, Berean Study Bible, BSB. Copyright ©2016 by Bible Hub. Used by permission. All rights reserved Worldwide.

Scripture quotations marked (ESV) are taken from The ESV® Bible (The Holy Bible, English Standard Version®) copyright © 2001 by Crossway, a publishing ministry of Good News Publishers. ESV® Text Edition: 2011. Used by permission. All rights reserved.

Scripture quotations marked (KJV) are taken from the King James Bible. Accessed on Bible Gateway. www.BibleGateway.com.

Scripture quotations marked (NASB) are taken from the New American Standard Bible ® (NASB), copyright © 1960, 1962, 1963, 1968, 1971, 1972, 1973, 1975, 1977, 1995 by The Lockman Foundation. Used by permission. www.Lockman.org.

Scripture quotations marked (NIV) are taken from the Holy Bible, New International Version. Copyright © 1973, 1978, 1984, 2011 by Biblica, Inc.® Used by permission. All rights reserved worldwide.

Scripture quotations marked (NKJV) are taken from the New King James Version®. Copyright © 1982 by Thomas Nelson, Inc. Used by permission. All rights reserved.

Scripture quotations marked (NLT) are taken from the Holy Bible, New Living Translation, copyright © 1996, 2004, 2015 by Tyndale House Foundation. Used by permission of Tyndale House Publishers, Inc., Carol Stream, Illinois 60188. All rights reserved.

Scripture quotations marked (NRSV) are taken from the New Revised Standard Version Bible, copyright © 1989 the Division of Christian Education of the National Council of the Churches of Christ in the United States of America. Used by permission. All rights reserved.

Cover Design and text layout: www.studionamedbermudez.com

Published by Completely You 365, LLC

We Deliver Potential. ®

ISBN: 9798640975062

#COMPLETELYMARRIED

Dedication

This book is dedicated to our father, Reverend John A. Nash, who passed away from a two-and-a-half-year battle with colon cancer. He dedicated over thirty years to counseling married couples. Our father poured out everything he had until the last breath, and we humbly take up his torch and continue his legacy of pouring into individuals and couples to help them do relationships God's way. He always said, "My ceiling is your floor." We love you, Dad!

—Damien and Kenady

Table of Contents

Foreword by Darius and Melba Dunson 12

Introduction: How We Met — His and Her Side of the Story 15

PART 1: Foundations for Courtship 31

Chapter 1: Accountability 33

Chapter 2: Boundaries 49

Chapter 3: Vision 55

PART 2: Courtship Journey 67

Chapter 4: The Beginning Stages of Courtship 69

Chapter 5: Maintaining Your Other Relationships 81

Chapter 6: The Courtship Journey Continues— No Plan B 89

Chapter 7: Transitions—From Courting To Engaged 99

Chapter 8: Premarital Counseling— Setting up your Marriage For Success 115

PART 3: A Biblical Understanding of Marriage 121

Chapter 9: Back To The Original State 123

Chapter 10: The Beauty Of Covenant 135

Chapter 11: Leading and Submitting 147

Chapter 12: How To Prepare To Be A Husband 155

Chapter 13: How To Prepare To Be A Wife 175

PART 4: *To The Altar and Beyond* *193*

    Chapter 14: *Planning Your Wedding* *195*

    Chapter 15: *Wedding Day* *201*

    Chapter 16: *You're Married Now—What's Next?* *207*

About The Authors *217*

Acknowledgments *218*

References: Works Cited *222*

References: Works Consulted *224*

Foreword
by Darius and Melba Dunson

We had our first opportunity to sit down for breakfast at a local restaurant and have a chat with Damien and Kenady during the pre-married stage of their relationship. We had a great time together, full of real conversation about their relationship and who they were. They were vibrant, fun, and full of jokes. We won't say who, but one of us had an extra stash of shredded cheese in his or her pocket to add to the grits—and then topped it off with a freestyle rap song about the "need for cheese." Needless to say, we could not contain the laughter! That was the moment we realized these two would cultivate an enjoyable and safe space to do life together.

Very seldom do we come across a couple with wisdom beyond their years, who value transparency and vulnerability as much as they value fun and laughter. They are truly a unique couple with a heart for God and a desire to see people grow to their fullest potential, experiencing wholeness as individuals in their relationship with God and in their relationships with others. We have had the privilege of walking with them through the courtship process, providing premarital counseling, and now seeing them flourish as a married couple.

During our time with them, it became evident that Damien and Kenady have the ability to communicate important principles in relevant, authentic ways that are memorable and applicable. God has been imparting words and revelation regarding relationships to Damien for years, and it has been an honor to witness the transference of those experiences into book format. From his previous work, *#CompletelySingle*, to this book in partnership with Kenady, *#CompletelyMarried*, we get the opportunity to see multiple sides of the spectrum: single (the struggle and the strides), engaged (the hunt and the hard work), and married (the beginning and beyond).

#CompletelyMarried is true to form, as it represents all that we love about the Nashes. It is a blueprint for how to establish a solid foundation upon which you can build in your marriage. This book is a must-read that provides Bible-based insight for newlyweds and for those who are seasoned from years of marriage. With over twenty-three years of experience in our own marriage, we can affirm that many principles they have shared are the same principles that have kept our marriage flourishing. The joy and passion of their union shine through on every page and will inspire you to rekindle the passion God intended for marriages.

The future is so bright for this amazing couple! This is the first of many books that they will author together. We foresee them serving the body of Christ, and providing insight into marriage and dating, for years to come.

—*Pastors Darius and Melba Dunson, Victory Church*

#COMPLETELYMARRIED

Introduction:
How We Met—His and Her Side of the Story

As we begin the book, we feel it's important to share the story of how we met. We each give our respective account of what happened, but one thing is undeniable: God orchestrated our love story! Then we present the six stages of relationships as a framework for understanding what a healthy path for a God-centered relationship looks like. Now, let the storytelling begin.

His Side of the Story

This is where I (Damien) am supposed to write my side of the story on how we met. Now, in the process of co-writing this chapter, Kenady and I cannot see each other's story, so I am eager and intrigued to see what Kenady wrote about me.

My side of the story starts in July of 2017, when I traveled to Rome, Italy, with our church's young adult ministry, Fusion. Getting to that point was a journey in itself: I got into three accidents within the four months before I set foot on the plane to Italy. I know—crazy, right? Nonetheless, I went and had a blast. I learned so much from meeting with young adults from all over the world. The cornerstone of my experience was getting comfortable with sharing the gospel of Jesus Christ.

On the second-to-last day of the trip, we attended a big concert with Montell Jordan (you know his song, "This is how we do it!"), who is one of the worship leaders at our church. It was an amazing night of worship, and over three hundred people raised their hands to receive Christ. I was headed back to my tour bus around midnight when my leaders rushed over to me. They said, "Hey, ▆▆▆ is acting weird. Can you come and help us out?"

I walked up to our friend, who was in a daze. She seemed drunk. After she spoke a couple of words, her look into my eyes was my confirmation: she was under the influence of a demonic presence. This trip had just gotten real. When we tried to get her to the bus, she ended up wandering aimlessly through the crowd. It was scary!

I started to rebuke the demonic spirit in front of the crowd. Next thing you knew, she had turned to me and thrown a punch. I leaned back as the first punch missed. "This woman just swung at me!" I thought. I was definitely taken off guard. Then *boom!* Like Mayweather, she sucker-punched me right in my left rib cage. That young lady hit me in my rib so hard, both my breath and my pride ran out of me like Usain Bolt in the 100-meter dash—gone.

I was stunned, but I still felt the need to protect our friend. This was not her. After several hours, we got her some help, though there were some steps that had to be taken to protect the rest of the team. We all returned home safely, but in the back of my mind, there was still a nagging question unanswered.

By now, I know you are asking, "What does this have to do with meeting Kenady?" Stick with me—we will get to that in a second!

Several days later, I was recalling my crazy Rome story to a business partner and mentor when he asked me, "Damien, how was Eve created?" After I thought about it, I said, "God removed a rib from Adam." My mentor replied, "I believe God is about to do something in the area with your wife."

I want to be transparent here. For years, my "rib" had been a source of silent frustration. Have you ever been frustrated in an area of your life, particularly about finding a spouse (or being found by one)? Maybe you are like I was, yearning for love and companionship, silently asking God to bring somebody in your life. This desire also created a porn addiction, which I battled for several years, even with help from my accountability partner (a.k.a., my "accountability"). Praise God, He delivered me after years of addiction. However, my accountability would also hear countless stories of my longing for someone with whom I could celebrate life's accomplishments—cheering each other on and growing together.

But I didn't want to bombard God with my selfish prayers, so I decided to focus on my purpose. One thing that did bring me a little solace was the revelation that Jesus has waited more than two thousand years for His bride. Why can't we wait ten, twenty, or even thirty years?

I also wanted to see if anybody in the Bible had experienced a season of frustration or a frustrating situation to which I could relate. After hearing a pastor talk about Paul's struggles in Acts, I studied this story for myself and was floored—because his story matched mine:

> After we were brought safely through, we then learned that the island was called Malta. The native people showed us unusual kindness, for they kindled a fire and welcomed us all, because it had begun to rain and was cold. When Paul had gathered a bundle of sticks and put them on the fire, a viper came out because of the heat and fastened on his hand. When the native people saw the creature hanging from his hand, they said to one another, "No doubt this man is a murderer. Though he has escaped from the sea, Justice has not allowed him to live." He, however, shook off the creature into the fire and suffered no harm. They were waiting for him to swell up or suddenly fall down dead. But when they had waited a long time and saw no misfortune come to him, they changed their minds and said that he was a god.
>
> Now in the neighborhood of that place were lands belonging to the chief man of the island, named Publius, who received us and entertained us hospitably for three days. It happened that the father of Publius lay sick with fever and dysentery. And Paul visited him and prayed, and putting his hands on him, healed him. And when this had taken place, the rest of the people on the island who had diseases also came and were cured. They also honored us greatly, and when we were about to sail, they put on board whatever we needed.
>
> —Acts 28:1–10 (ESV)

If you continue reading, you find that Paul and his crew landed on Malta after being shipwrecked. They didn't quite make it to their intended destination, Rome. (Remember that I had gotten into three wrecks myself trying to get to Rome.) Paul was positioning himself to serve the people of Malta by gathering sticks when a snake bit him on his hand. As the people saw this, they accused him of being a murderer. After he shook the snake off and nothing happened to him, however, the people called him a god. The moral of this particular section of the story is that you can't trust people's opinions of you. In one breath, they will praise you, and in the next, they can curse you. Put your trust in God and God alone.

After being on the island for three days, the story says, Publius's father was sick with a fever and dysentery, which is an infection in the intestines.[1] Paul visited the man, laid his hands on him, and healed him. After Paul healed Publius's father through the power of God, the people on the island caught wind of it. Then the rest of the people came and were cured. I just love the Bible!

But did you see what I saw? I am often guilty of reading the Bible so fast that I miss the revelation. Paul could have focused on the snake bite on his hand. Sometimes the pain enters our lives unexpectedly, like when the young lady hit me in the ribs. You might be dealing with the unexpected death of someone close to you. You might have been laid off recently or had an unexpected breakup. You might feel like someone bit you (or hit you). I know exactly what you are going through. However, God urges us to realize that there is a purpose in the pain and that we don't need to focus on it. Paul was not frustrated by the bite, as we see in the story. He later used those same hands that were bitten by the viper to heal Publius's father through the power of the Holy Spirit.

I decided not to focus on the hit anymore. The enemy wanted me to focus on the pain and frustration. I learned that the enemy will try to break what God is trying to bring into your life, but you must reply, "Not today, Satan!" I believe this situation catapulted me to the next level spiritually, as my wife and I are going to heal people through our ministry, nationally and globally, by the power of the Holy Spirit.

After this amazing revelation, I was on the search. The Bible speaks of "he who finds a wife" (Proverbs 18:22), so I had to start looking for wifey material. I knew my rib would be around the corner, I just knew it, and my older brother David even mentioned to me that God told him my wife was around the corner. (Note, not everybody can speak into your life in this way. Sometimes you have to vet an individual—and move on if they have not shown any spiritual fruit in their own life.)

I had found myself attracted to two particular women on my Rome trip, one from our church and another who was from another country. I told my friends that I was trying to reach out to both of these women and see what happened. After several attempts and failures, however, something just did not bode well with either of these women and it was time to move on.

In February 2018, I started noticing Kenady posting on Facebook. I knew Kenady already but had not been thinking of her in that fashion. In fact, every time I would think about her, I wanted to laugh. For the last three to four years, she would sit behind me at church. I would try to say something to her quickly, we would share a laugh, and I would turn around. I could tell she was a little nervous or intimidated, so I didn't want to make it awkward for her. Thus, I would cut our interactions short. But I finally slid back into her DM, or direct messages, a couple of days after my birthday, on Facebook Instant Messenger, to make a joke about her new headshot. "Why you stealing people's headshots from Google?" I think I said.

She responded so quickly that it seemed like she had been waiting on me to talk to her. She was hungry! (Of course, this is only my side of the story.) My friend Justin would always coach me, "Just try to keep the conversation going and see if she continues to respond." And I tell you what, that is what started to happen. Kenady kept on hitting me back.

After about two weeks of this, I manned up and challenged myself, "Bruh, you have to ask her for the number." So that's what I did: I contacted her again and asked her for her number. But this time, she did not respond. Crickets, I tell you—crickets. I thought to myself, "Okay, what did I say wrong?" Then, after a while, she wrote me back and denied my request and advance. I told myself to keep cool. You never want to seem desperate or like you're losing your swag. So I told her I understood and didn't need her number at that time. I am patient, and this was not my first rodeo.

Over the next couple of days, as we continued to talk via Messenger, we discussed our favorite scriptures. She mentioned a scripture in Hebrews, and this gave me an idea. I had been telling my friends about a devotional on John 21, and they were being blessed by it, so I sent Kenady a message late one night and told her that I had a scripture to share. She replied that she was ready for me to type it out. Then I told her that it was *waaay* too long for me to type out, so I would need to call her. She pointed out that I didn't have her number, but I replied with a screenshot of the Instant Messenger phone icon and replied, "I don't need your phone number to call you." I was a savage, I know! I think I might have called her the night after, and that was the call that did it. She fell in love with me that night.

One of the first things she asked me after the devotion was what my intentions were with her. She wanted me to man the heck up, which I found attractive. We talked some more that night, and she shared her doubts about a relationship with me. She also admitted that she had bitten off all her nails when I'd asked for her number, which was the reason for the long pause. I still don't know why she did that. She mentioned that I was known as the demon slayer at our church and it's intimidating to be with such a person. Our age difference was a concern for her as well. And lastly, she mentioned that she had baggage, to which I replied, "Is it Hartsfield-Jackson baggage?"—referring to the large number of bags that comes through Hartsfield-Jackson Atlanta International, the busiest airport in the world.

I continued, "We all have baggage, but the real question is, are we going to use our baggage to sabotage the relationship?" I asked her if she intended to do that, and she said no. I told her I understood her concerns and then asked her, "So, what do you want to do?" She turned it back on me: "So what do you want to do?" I finally answered, "Well, it's late, so you are going to go to bed and I am going to call you tomorrow because I want to. Is that all right with you?" She said yes, and I hung up the phone like a man.

We didn't waste any time, and our friendship stage went quickly. I am now a believer in the idea that when you know, you know, because after a few conversations, I simply knew that she was the lady for me. Still, there was no rush. I gave her my book #CompletelySingle so we could be on the same page together. She read that book quickly, and guess what? She fell in love again. And don't get it twisted: I was smitten with her, too.

I told Kenady at the tail end of one conversation, "I am not trying to manipulate you. Matter of fact, I am not trying to have sex with you. I'm a virgin, anyways. I don't care about that stuff. All I want to do is continue to pursue God's heart and yours." Purity was at the forefront of the friendship. "I am the protector of your heart," I told her once.

"I decide what comes in. I am on the wall, and I am mandated to fend off anything that tries to come in."

After that, Kenady said she was fighting, liking me. She told me she had been fighting me inside her head and heart, telling herself she didn't like me. But one day—it was March 25—she had to be honest and finally told me she liked me. Her accountability knew me and liked me for Kenady, as well, telling her, "You know that is your husband." Kenady told me she realized that she would be stupid to try to sabotage this relationship. She also said that my purity gave her security and that she felt loved even though I hadn't touched her.

Right before we got together officially, she wanted to tell me about her past. One day she will share it with the world, and I will be right there, cheering her on. Yes, it was a tough story to hear, but it was necessary. My reaction was minimal. I told her Christ's blood covers it all and I wanted to be the best representation of Christ in her life. Therefore, I accepted her just as she was and told her we were not going back there ever again. I said, "I don't care if you are not a virgin. Just don't put yourself in that situation again. And with me, you are not going to do that stuff anyways until after marriage. Our sacrifice now will help us in the future." I told her that my goal was to present her at the altar one day without any spot, wrinkle, or blemish.

April 7, 2018, was the first day we sat together at church, which felt so real and natural. Later in the book, you will understand why this date was so important. But now, it's Kenady's turn to tell her side of the story.

Her Side of the Story (The Right-er Side)

There are always two sides to a story. Both sides can be right, but one side is usually *more* right, which I'd argue is the female's side. Our story begins with a certain somebody sliding into another person's direct message, or DM. I will let you be the one to decide who was sliding into whose DM, but before we get to that part of the story, let me offer you a little prelude.

After I graduated college and moved back home, my older sister introduced me to the young adult ministry at Victory World Church, called Fusion. In January 2014, we both got connected and joined a small group called Transformers, which changed my life. It was amazing to be around a group of young adults who were living a fun and authentic life for Christ. My small group leader at the time thought that I would be a great leader. To be honest, I was afraid to step up because I didn't feel like I was worthy of leading. I was a hot mess, dealing with a lot of baggage from college and past relationships. However, I "woman'd up," as Damien would put it. I overcame my fears and answered the call to leadership. Later in the summer of 2014, I joined the Fusion leadership team. I decided to get re-baptized and publicly declare my rededication to Jesus.

Shortly after that, I began to have demonic dreams. I remember sharing in the Fusion leader GroupMe about a dream I'd had. Damien, who was the leader of the prayer team for Fusion at the time, decided to DM me with his concerns about the dream I'd described. Damien's nickname was "the Demon Slayer," so it was no surprise that he came ready to slay whatever demon I might be facing. He proceeded to give me advice on spiritual warfare and how to guard my spirit.

Over my season of Fusion leadership, we served together during various outreaches. Honestly, we never noticed each other "like that."

We were just there to serve the Lord and not to try to find a significant other. We would see each other in passing, crack jokes, and have brief conversations here and there. He slid into my DMs every so often, too, asking if I'd had any more demonic dreams. I also sat behind him during Saturday night services at Victory, though never intentionally: the area where I preferred to sit just so happened to be near where he preferred to sit.

In fact, I was afraid of Damien. I thought that he would see some evil spirit in me and be ready to cast it out of me because this man, I recognized, was truly a modern-day Paul. There had been a few times when I had gone up for prayer and Damien ended up being the next person available. His prayers would either have me ugly-face crying or on the floor, literally. I remember one time, specifically, when I went down for prayer and again, Damien was the next person open, so I approached him and told him that I needed prayer for fear. He began to pray in the Spirit, and the first words that came out of his mouth were so specific to what I was going through, it astounded me. I hadn't talked to anybody about it at the time. Immediately, I collapsed in the chair and wept. He proceeded to pray over me, nailing every area with which I was struggling. It was truly supernatural. When the prayer ended, I opened my eyes, and the first thing I saw was him on bended knee. I jerked back and was so weirded out by that. Though I had some fleeting sense that this was foreshadowing things to come, I just brushed it off and didn't think anything else of it. Never in a million years would I have thought he'd be the one I would marry.

Now fast-forward to February of 2018, when the DM of all DMs took place. Damien slid into my Facebook inbox, cracking a joke about one of my photos. Unlike the other times when we had randomly talked in private messages, I noticed that this time, we were at almost two weeks of going back and forth in the conversation. I remember telling my older sister, "Um, I think Damien likes me, and is pursuing me for some reason, because he keeps messaging me on Facebook." She asked me, "Well, do you like him like that?" I told her no, I didn't think so. She responded, "Well, why are you messaging him back?" I couldn't answer her.

Shortly after my conversation with my sister, Damien messaged me and said, "I usually do this in person, but I don't know when I will see you again. We have been messaging each other for a while now, and I wanted to know if I can get your number so we can get to know each other a little more." Do you want to know what I did when I read that message? I closed out of Facebook and bit off all of my nails out of nervousness. I knew he saw that I'd read his message, and I usually responded pretty quickly, but this was one question I could not answer. I contemplated deleting Facebook altogether to avoid answering his question. Not to sound full of myself, but I had turned down plenty of guys in the past when they'd asked for my number. This time was not so easy. Part of me couldn't say no, but the other part couldn't say yes. A few hours later, I messaged him and told him that I was too nervous to give him my number and had multiple reasons why I couldn't. Guess how this man responded? He said, "It's cool. I totally understand. I don't need your number to be able to talk to you. I can just hit the phone button at the corner and call you via Facebook audio." The audacity! I was totally baffled and felt like he'd one-up'd me. I hadn't even known you could do that. Eventually, he did indeed call me via Facebook, and guess what I did? I answered.

The first time he called me, he told me about a study he'd done on John 21:1–17. I might not have fallen head-over-heels in love with him that day, but the way he broke down the Word and the depth of the revelation he had were extremely attractive to me. I'd never met a man so on fire for God and truly after His own heart. After Damien had lured me in with the Bible study, I told him the reasons why I felt like I couldn't give him my number. The excuses ranged from him being six years older than me to my fear of being with someone who slays demons. I know I sound like a crazy person, not wanting to be with someone who is walking in His gift and doing what God has called him to do, yet I was honestly terrified at the prospect of being with someone like that. Unfazed by my excuses, he told me he appreciated me being honest with him. He proceeded to tell me that he still wanted to get to know me more and was still going to call me, if that was okay with me. So he continued to do just that, calling me via Facebook, and you best believe I continued to answer.

I prayed to God, "If this is who You have for me, then change my heart." I kid you not, within a few short days, I was no longer trying to run from him, but found myself falling for him, instead. I realized that I had a past history of hunkering down in chaos yet fleeing from order. I constantly tried to push Damien away and talk down about myself. I wanted him to stop pursuing me and was afraid to be with him because I was running from my calling. I knew that being with a man of God like Damien, I could no longer play it safe, make excuses, and live an ordinary Christian life. I also didn't feel like I was a strong enough woman to be with such a strong man of God—but He quickly removed that lie from my head.

When I came to my senses, I realized I would be stupid to sabotage this potential relationship. Damien was everything I had prayed to God to find in a man. Damien is a unicorn. These days, how many men in their mid-thirties are virgins, fully surrendered to God, lovers of accountability, and walking in the power of the Holy Spirit? I'm not saying they aren't out there, but I tell you, there ain't one on every block. So I decided to stop trying to run and to accept the godly pursuit. From the beginning of my friendship with Damien, God has been healing me in so many areas, including fears, insecurities, and self-doubt. Oftentimes, we think we have to have it all together before we enter into a relationship, but the truth of the matter is, God will use a significant other to continue the sanctification process on a new level. Damien is not my savior, but he has definitely been a vessel my Savior has used in my life. I am so grateful that Damien slid into my DM!

With that being said, I want to give a message to the fellas: DM could also stand for Divine Moment. You'd better take advantage of that moment and slide into her DM if led by the Lord. She might just be your missing rib! And to my sisters: Don't always Christian "curve" that man of God in your inbox. He just might be your Boaz!

Takeaways from Both Sides

You have read both sides of the beginning of our story now, and we hope you enjoyed it. We were definitely blessed to write it for you! Here are several takeaways before we get into the rest of the book.

Know your own worth. Yes, Kenady had been around me (Damien) for several years, but I never really saw her worth until I realized my own. This was key for me as I went into my season of finding a wife: I had to understand what I brought to the table, first and foremost, before inviting another person to dine with me.

Use your head—observe the fruit. Secondly, we suggest you use your head *before* your heart is fully in the relationship. You will be able to see if the partnership is going to be fruitful or not by looking at how the other person has already affected the people around him or her.

Let peace be one of your guides. I (Damien) experienced supernatural peace with Kenady. After she said yes to our friendship, I saw her countenance start to change, and fear and intimidation started to be non-issues. That brought me peace so that I wasn't anxious at all. I just wanted to discover, more and more, about this woman God had placed in front of me.

The Stages of a Relationship

Understanding the stages of a relationship can help keep that discovery process healthy and God-focused. Below are the steps to a healthy heterosexual relationship, in the order they should flow when you're courting your partner. I learned about these steps in my late twenties and early thirties. Our mother, Jeanne "Kathy" Nash, developed the category descriptions below, and she has allowed us to include them in our book. Though not every relationship will look exactly like this, the main takeaway is that there should be order, purpose, and intentionality when courting. We don't want any more confusion, manipulation, or wasted time to befall any single person who reads this book! This can also be used as a resource to train your children or mentees who may come into your life.

Exploration

Christians will seek to find potential dating partners at church, through friends, at work, or online (cautiously). They will look for commonality in each other's interests and hobbies. They will dress with modesty. Their conversation or communication will be reflective of Christ.

Friendship

Christians will relate to each other based on mutual interests and seek to get involved in group activities with other Christian friends. They may do ministry projects together. In the friendship stage, there is no need for exclusivity, meaning the individuals are able to befriend others of the opposite sex in the context of godly relationships. Each person may want to find out information about the other person's family. The couple (who are still friends) should avoid both physical intimacy and meeting in secluded locations.

Committed

The couple will agree to explore whether this is to be a long-term relationship. Minor males should ask the girl's parents (Guardians) for permission to date their daughter. Emphasis will be on building each other's character. They will attend Christian conferences, listen to Christian material, read Christian books, and watch Christian videos. The two will attend special family events such as reunions and weddings. They will continue to avoid physical intimacy and meeting in secluded locations. They should not use the bedroom to converse and entertain one another. The pair **shouldn't** be open to dating others. They have agreed to date with a purpose and intentionality, which is called courtship. The pair should avoid buying expensive gifts for one another or one taking on the other's financial obligations.

Pre-Engagement

The couple should discuss specific areas to determine compatibility. Disclosure should be made about major debt, health issues, desired number of children, home ownership, etc. The non-negotiables should be discussed. The couple should receive premarital counseling or classes to help determine if it is God's will for them to marry. It would be beneficial for both to complete a temperament inventory or other assessments to determine areas of strengths and possible difficulties in their union. The pair should remain celibate. The man should ask permission of the woman's parents (or guardians) to marry their daughter.

Engagement

The couple should set the budget for the wedding and stick to it. If they are having a public wedding, they should consider designing the ceremony with a memorable theme so attendees will have a renewed appreciation for God's design for marriage. They should also continue premarital counseling, or begin it if they have not done so already. The couple should avoid moving in together or joining finances. They should remain celibate.

Marriage (or Not)

Let us make this very clear for you: your whole goal in entering into a relationship with the opposite sex is to glorify God and bring Him joy. After that, it's to see if God is calling you two to be married. Now, at any stage, you have the right and choice to walk away if you do not feel that God is calling you to be married. You don't have to wait until a ring is bought and the wedding is planned and halfway paid for. This is a serious commitment, and accordingly, you should go into marriage with the mindset that divorce is never an option. Marriage is a beautiful thing! It takes work, but it is worth every second when it's done right and in order.

Now that we have established the order or progression of a relationship, let's begin the journey to the altar and beyond. Buckle your seatbelts and enjoy the book!

Part 1:
Foundations for Courtship

#COMPLETELYMARRIED

Chapter 1:
Accountability

You may wonder why we're starting off this book by talking about accountability. Well, we believe it is important to start thinking about accountability before even entering into a courtship or dating relationship. It's so easy to get distracted with the lovey-dovey phase and postpone accountability until down the road, once you are already well into a committed relationship. However, you may be more tempted, and might even fall into sin, when there isn't anyone "all up in your business." We encourage you to find accountability as soon as possible to help you build a solid foundation—and avoid having to backtrack and possibly undo a lot of damage. Accountability can save you time, emotional hardship, and unnecessary problems helping you navigate your relationship in a healthy and godly way. In this chapter, we will share how we went about finding accountability, what the accountability sessions entailed, and what traits to look for when finding an accountability couple.

Choosing Our Accountability Couple

What do you feel when someone mentions "accountability"? I (Damien) know when I first heard the word, I got nervous. My hands started to get moist, my heart started to pound just a tad bit harder, and questions started rollerblading through my mind. What if they knew X, Y, or Z about me? Should I be honest and fully transparent?

Accountability Defined

Being honest is not a bad place to start in any accountability relationship. However, if you want to go deeper and grow in maturity as a disciple, you will start to be transparent. Transparency is being intentional about sharing things with which you are struggling. The people to whom you open up should be willing to see past your confessions so you can receive the necessary advice or healing God is seeking to bring into your life. Please keep this in your mind as we dissect what true, godly accountability looks like.

Now, it took us a couple of weeks to decide on our accountability couple. We established some criteria before choosing. My first thought was Pastor Darius and Melba Dunson, who are leaders at our church in Atlanta. After they were guests on my radio program *Midnight Breakfast*, and did an amazing job, I knew I wanted them on my accountability team. I didn't know how to ask them, however, and I didn't know if that was what Kenady wanted as well. But in fact, when I asked her if there was a couple she had in mind, she said, "*Shoooot*, I want the Dunsons." I knew she was the one! We knew they were extremely busy, though, and we wanted a couple who could dedicate more time for us, so we agreed to ask a younger couple first. We ideally wanted a couple who had been married for at least five years, who had a model marriage, and with whom we were both comfortable. Right away, we thought of Justin and Jasmine Hart. It would be an easy transition for me because Justin and I were already close.

Webster states that accountability is "an obligation or willingness to accept responsibility or to account for one's actions."[2] One of my past mentees taught me that you have to define the terms of the accountability relationship by asking yourself two questions: (1) Who am I willing to be accountable *to*, and (2) who am I accountable *for*? Because there is a big difference.

Picking an accountability couple can be tough, but you must take the initiative—so that's what we did. We reached out and asked the couple to whom we wanted to be accountable. You see, you don't *have* to have accountability; you *get* to have accountability! It's a gift, not a limitation.

Very early in our relationship, before accountability, we started developing "checkpoints" in our conversations. This is where you ask each other: "How are you doing?" "How do you think we're doing?" "What can I do better?" This way, you get to learn what the other person thinks about the relationship. Even though you might think everything is fine and dandy, the other person might voice something different. This is not a time to get defensive or offended, but a time to learn how to communicate. Adding weekly "checkpoints" into your conversation prior to choosing your accountability couple helps you learn how to communicate with your accountability when they ask you questions at your scheduled monthly meeting.

The Character of Your Accountability

So, how do you find an accountability partner or couple? Certain qualities are especially important in looking for accountability. I (Damien) had the privilege of drafting a curriculum proposal for our church's singles ministry, which identifies five essential characteristics that you yourself should possess for a successful, healthy accountability relationship. However, as I prayed about it, God pointed me to two additional, necessary qualities to look for in the character of your accountability.

Intentionality is a quality that you will continue to hear us talk about throughout the book. If something in your life is ungodly, an accountability partner is intentional to try to help you get rid of it as soon as possible. Such things could include toxic relationships, unhealthy habits, or destructive addictions like porn. If you have a serious problem, this person will help keep you accountable and will check on you—for instance, by setting safeguards on your computer or any other electronic device that has internet access. You yourself can be intentional and set relevant notifications to send directly to your accountability. The goal is to bring problems out into the open to avoid allowing the enemy a foothold.

Vulnerability is a key ingredient in your accountability relationships. Again, it goes both ways. You are exposing yourself to potential hurt, which is necessary if you want to experience growth in relationships. God desires for us to be vulnerable with Him so we can receive the help or healing He intends for *all* of us. However, He operates on the basis of our free will—it's His gift to us—so He won't bless or heal us if we don't allow it, nor will He bless or heal the person we're merely *pretending* to be.

So, how can we become more vulnerable with those we are in community with, and especially those to whom we are accountable? First, by practicing how to be authentic. As we used to say back when I (Damien) was a teenager, "just be real." When you open up to someone for accountability purposes, be respectful but don't sugarcoat. That said, there is a time and a place for private information to be revealed. If it is sensitive, please use discretion. Women should avoid sharing intimate things with men, especially if the relationship is either in the friendship stage or early in courtship. This goes for men sharing with women as well. You don't want to create unnecessary soul-ties early. You should intentionally reserve intimate conversations for your same-sex accountability. This is why they are in your life! Though, never feel pressured to share, either, except as God leads you. Again, this is why an intimate relationship with the Spirit of God is important as you walk with Him throughout your life.

Secondly, practice being transparent. Transparency is when you are able to see through an object. Your accountability can only help you with the things you share! It should not have to be an interrogation every time you talk or meet up. Your accountability may have to lead in this area at first, however, so you can see how it's done.

Active listening is a vital component of your accountability's character. You should desire a person who can listen without jumping to conclusions. As James 1:19 says, "My dear brothers and sisters, take note of this: Everyone should be quick to listen, slow to speak and slow to become angry" (NIV). I remember my grandmother would say, "I know you heard me, but did you listen to what I said?" Hearing is a gift from God, but listening is a skill that can be developed. It involves focus, concentration, and intentionality. Sometimes we have to position our accountability meetings in quiet locations so we can remove all distractions. Your accountability should also ask the right questions for better understanding.

After I (Damien) came back from my trip to Rome, I told Justin how perverted the spirit was over there. One night, we walked right past a stretch of homosexual clubs, where hundreds of people stood outside making out with each other—men kissing men and women kissing women. Well, those images were impressed upon all of us. I went back to my room and started to have dreams about homosexual relationships. It was something I hadn't ever experienced in my life to that magnitude. I told Justin this, and he didn't make assumptions or judge, but simply listened. My trust in his leadership and accountability increased as a result. We prayed, and it was never brought up again, nor have I struggled with those sorts of thoughts or dreams since. We need more believers to develop active listening skills!

Reachability describes the ease with which someone can contact you, connect with you, or influence you. Your accountability needs to be reachable in two ways. First, you need to be allowed to contact him or her. Communication in an accountability relationship should be a two-way street, and although you can't expect to be in touch 24/7, it can strain the relationship if your accountability is never around or is not accessible. Secondly, your accountability needs to be in the Word of God so that what they say carries biblical weight and has an impression on your soul. In other words, your accountability should be bearing some kind of spiritual fruit that is evident and convincing.

Grace and truth are things we have learned that most accountability must provide to help us remain humble. John 1:14 (NIV) says, "The Word became flesh and made his dwelling among us. We have seen his glory, the glory of the one and only Son, who came from the Father, full of *grace* and *truth*" (emphasis added). To have an understanding of this, your main accountability must be saved. Moreover, they should bring grace and truth by *constructive correction*. When they bring grace and truth into the mix, it builds trust. We can bring deeper issues to our accountability because they are ready and available to respond with the Word, not merely their own words. Their response should not be judgmental and condemning, either. Matthew 7:1–2 says, "Do not judge, or you too will be judged. For in the same way you judge others, you will be judged, and with the measure you use, it will be measured to you" (NIV). Constructive correction from your accountability is based on the Word of God, not their feelings. You need friends, especially accountability, to know the Word and use it not to manipulate you, but to bring you back to God, if you have thought or are thinking about tiptoeing into sin. Accordingly, you want your accountability to feel comfortable telling you the truth. If you want a friend to be your accountability, make sure that friend will speak the truth in love, even if it may hurt your feelings or step on your toes.

Caring and loving may sound elementary, but they are crucial in a relationship, including an accountability relationship. In 2016, my (Damien's) father was diagnosed with stage four cancer, and it began one of the toughest seasons in my life. My community and my accountability called and checked up on me during this time. This was vital because sometimes those who are hurting or in a dry season tend to isolate themselves, whether by instinct or so they don't feel like a burden. However, the body of Christ sharing their love and care for me personally was one key factor that kept me at my local church during that season. First John 4:21 says, "And he has given us this command: Anyone who loves God must also love their brother and sister" (NIV). We must love—and show love.

Baptism of the Spirit is by far the most important of this list. God gave His Son Jesus as a gift to the world; however, Jesus gave the church the Holy Spirit. It a blessing to receive the baptism of the Spirit that brings power. If someone is not baptized by the Spirit of God, how can they bring true accountability, with active listening, grace and truth, and boldness to call out things that are not of God in our lives? Acts 1:8 says, "But you will receive power when the Holy Spirit has come upon you; and you shall be My witnesses both in Jerusalem, and in all Judea and Samaria, and even to the remotest part of the earth" (NASB). When I was first baptized in the Holy Spirit in my room in college, I thought nothing of this, but as I've gained more understanding, the baptism of the Spirit has brought me peace in making life decisions.

We write all of these things not just so you can interview prospective accountability partners and say, "If you don't have these qualities, you can't hold me accountable." No, we also want you to desire these characteristics yourself so *you* can hold someone else accountable one day. Ultimately, you and your accountability should both possess these things so you can better
serve each other.

What Accountability Meetings Looks Like

Now that you have an idea of what an accountability couple should look like in their character, we will provide a blueprint for what an accountability meeting might look like. Below, we present you with an outline of our first two meetings so you can get an idea of what to expect or, if you are the accountability *for* another couple, you can get ideas for how to structure your sessions.

First Meeting (60 minutes)

1. *The proposal.* The first thing we did was officially ask Justin and Jasmine face to face if they would be our accountability couple. We told them why we wanted them to be our accountability. Write down what you are looking for in your accountability so you can make your expectations known to them and so they know how to handle the relationship. (And in case you were wondering, Justin and Jasmine said yes!)

Here was our list:
- The couple had to be Christians.
- The couple had to be married.
- The couple had to be serving God faithfully in church.
- The couple had to be married at least five years.
- The couple had to have a good track record (that is, a successful marriage).
- We had to agree on the couple.
- We had to feel comfortable with the couple.
- We had to believe the couple would be bold enough to correct us if we were out of line.

2. *Getting to know each other.* The accountability couple should start off with basic, introductory questions to build rapport: "Where were you born?" "Where were you raised?" "What school did you attend?" "How did you guys meet?" (Note: In our meeting, they focused this part on Kenady, because they already knew me, Damien.)

3. Going deeper. If time allows and everyone feels comfortable, the accountability couple can ask deeper questions, such as "What were your past relationships like?" It's important for the accountability couple to know about the other couple's past, not to use it against them but to understand where they have been and what struggles they may have faced. This knowledge of your background context will help your accountability promote success in your current relationship. It will better enable them to prepare to handle different concerns or challenges that may arise.

4. Understanding the couple. Your accountability may ask you questions like "What attracted you to each other?" Justin and Jasmine wanted us to focus on character here, more so than on physical attributes. They asked us to describe each other's character as well as our own.

5. Wisdom and next steps. They gave us their wisdom, as well as homework for us to work on until the next meeting. They spoke on the importance of communication in relationships. Then we were given the task to write out our boundaries and vision. Boundaries can be physical, emotional, and spiritual. We will list ours later in the book. We suggest you set up two separate dates and literally write down your boundaries and visions. Then both of you should sign and date the papers and send a copy of them back to your accountability for their records. Also, our accountability asked us to come with questions to ask them, too, since accountability should never be one-sided.

A couple of days after our first meeting, our accountability reached out and suggested a meeting once a month until we (Damien and Kenady) either decided to tie the knot or decided our relationship wasn't working out. You see, courtship with accountability is purposeful, but nobody knows if it will work out or not. That's why we needed accountability—to humble ourselves and benefit from another perspective on our relationship. If our courtship did not work out, my (Damien's) goal was for Kenady to leave a better woman. I wouldn't damage her relationship with God but enhance her relationship with God, for her future husband.

Justin and Jasmine also asked us if we wanted to meet face to face or over video chat. We chose to alternate monthly between those two options. Instant Messenger on Facebook has a group chat function that worked perfectly. The accountability couple can use either the same phone or (as long as they're in separate rooms to prevent feedback) different phones. You can use other apps for video chats as well. Our main point here is to advise you to be intentional and do whatever works best for everyone involved in order to maintain consistency.

Second Meeting (60 minutes)

1. Follow-up. Your accountability will get a feel of how things have been since the last meeting, and go over the homework from the previous meeting. Here is a chance for the couple to be open and transparent. Don't be afraid to dive deep with your answers. Several days before our second accountability meeting, Kenady and I went bowling. We approached the kiosk to enter our names after learning that we could bowl for free. We had two young children bowling with us, who were about two or three years old. When you are bowling with young children, the kiosk allows you to preset their names and whether or not they need bumpers. Bumpers are for inexperienced bowlers so they won't get discouraged when they constantly see their balls go into the gutter. Similarly, it's important that young couples don't end up in the gutter due to their bad behaviors or misguided actions. An accountability couple act as the bumpers to prevent gutter relationships! Justin and Jasmine explained their role as our bumpers and told us that we could only get as much as we put into the accountability relationship. Their desire was for us to be as open and honest as possible. They also mentioned that they were available to us as sounding boards, and as mediators if we had a fight.

2. **Lesson of the day.** Prior to our second meeting, Justin and Jasmine sent us a link to an article about communication for us to look over beforehand and be ready to discuss.[3] It's important for a couple to challenge the couple(s) they are holding accountable. Relevant books and articles, as well as YouTube videos of talks, conferences, and sermons, can assist a couple in growth. Remember, this is a two-way street, so as the couple receiving the accountability, you can also send articles and videos that will encourage your accountability couple. You are all in this thing together!

3. **Learning each other.** Justin and Jasmine asked about our love languages. If you haven't heard of the book *5 Love Languages* by Dr. Gary Chapman, we highly recommend reading it.[4] Kenady's primary love language is quality time, while mine is physical touch. The other three love languages are acts of service, affirmation of words, and receiving gifts. I (Damien) hadn't realized that there were needs attached to our love languages: acceptance, affection, appreciation, approval, attention, comfort, encouragement, respect, security,

and support. Justin and Jasmine explained that it was important for me to understand the needs behind the love languages so I could serve Kenady well and not neglect her. Lack of knowledge can sometimes lead us to overlook or dismiss our partner's deeper needs, but knowledge of Christ is a crucial foundation for every relationship. We individually picked the top three "deeper needs," for ourselves and then for each other, and wrote explanations for our choices. Then we compared our responses to see what we got right.

4. **Feedback.** We asked Justin and Jasmine where they thought we were after three months, from their perspective. We wanted to give them the opportunity to share any concerns they may have had thus far. In return, they wanted feedback from us, as well, to see how we thought the session went. Remember, use this accountability for growth. Don't despise correct or honest feedback!

5. **Take-home message.** Jasmine ended the meeting by saying, "Your emotional commitment should not supersede relational commitment. Relationship comes first." A lot of couples try to act married when they are still dating, which means doing married things. You will end up hurt every time. Take this journey to courtship slowly and with a sober mind so you will not be blinded by your emotions and infatuations.

Here are some other questions that can be asked during your accountability sessions, by either party:
- Are you reading and studying the Word of God?
- Are you sharing your faith as a couple?

- Have you avoided lustful content (in shows and movies, on the internet and social media, etc.)?
- Are you personally winning the battle against greed and materialism?
- How's your mental health?
- Are you taking care of your body, God's temple (exercise, sleep, healthy diet, etc.)?
- How is your overall spiritual walk?
- Have you been giving to the Lord (tithes, offering, almsgiving, etc.)?
- What frustrates you about your partner? (This is an expectation question, which is important to talk through early in the courtship.)
- Have you crossed any boundaries within the relationship? If so, how?
- Are you struggling with unforgiveness?
- Are there any concerns that you can see in our relationship?
- What are some other tools that can help us with communication?

These overviews and examples should give you a good foundation of expectations for accountability, whether you're initiating an accountability relationship or are helping other couples reach the altar in purity and peace. As we have learned, you can successfully cover one or two topics during each session as you start to get comfortable with each other and learn to be transparent. We encourage couples to take their time getting to know each other—the real person—because there are plenty of things to talk about. These sessions are a good measuring stick to see if you were created to join together as husband and wife. Other topics you can discuss during future sessions: family background, finances, dreams and goals, intimacy needs, and marriage expectations. Topics should be appropriate for the season and stage of courtship you are in. For example, we waited to have the sex talk until our last session before our wedding because it wouldn't have been wise to have that talk early in our courtship.

So, how often should you meet with your accountability? The answer to this question is based on the couple and/or the individual. We encourage you to be intentional in finding individual accountability of the same sex before you enter into a relationship, courtship, or engagement. Why? In part, so you can have a good routine already established, but also so you can develop discipline in being transparent with your accountability. For some individuals, accountability is on an as-needed basis, while for others—like me, Damien—it's important to meet every week. You have to decide what fits your schedule and life. We believe this foundational accountability habit helps when the accountability couple comes into place.

We encourage same-sex accountability because, as we have seen and heard, opposite-sex accountability typically becomes awkward or weird. It can turn into an unhealthy soul-tie, in which attraction grows and eventually entangles one or both individuals in sin.

We also want to encourage you to not feel like you are trapped in courtship. You are not bound until "I do." If you are feeling like this person isn't the one, don't hesitate to break it off. Also, if you are someone who is helping other couples, don't be afraid to speak up and share your concerns as to why you think they should not be together. The sobering truth is that not all courtships end in marriage. An end in courtship is not a failure, however, but a success to prevent you from having a miserable marriage or getting a divorce. Having accountability should help you navigate this journey, safely and intentionally—staying pure and not damaging each other.

#COMPLETELYMARRIED

Chapter 2:
Boundaries

When you think about boundaries, what comes to mind? Maybe you think of restrictions, rules, or somebody trying to take all your fun away, like I (Damien) used to think. However, if you are like I was, fun might mean seeing how close you can get to sin before actually crossing the line. Boundaries were challenging because I didn't have the right perspective on reality, which is that the devil and his minions exist and want you to fall. They will come at you in many deceptive ways to cloud your judgment and produce strategies for you to trip over boundary lines. Over and over, the devil will recite the infamous phrase "Did God really say…?" until you start questioning the Word that brings life. And when you do fall, the devil introduces you to shame and guilt, which smear your self-image and the person God has called you to be.

Boundaries are for our protection, especially regarding sex. I'm sure we all can agree that sexual temptation is real. Song of Solomon 8:4 says "not to awaken love until the time is right" (NLT), but unfortunately, many of us have already awakened it. However, we believe God is raising up a generation to walk in sexual purity. Despite our pasts, we can all surrender to God's design and cease crossing sexual boundaries, choosing instead to respect the rights of our future spouses. The key to purity is remembering that it's more about your relationship with God than about being right or wrong or not crossing boundaries. God's love and a relationship with Him outweigh considerations of your character or integrity for its own sake. If you start looking at yourself and thinking you're righteous because of your actions, you lose sight of the reality that it's God who gives you the strength for righteous action. Remember, it's not about the rule; it's about His love. We keep the boundaries because we love God and the other person.

For us, Damien and Kenady, boundaries have been the catalyst of peace. It has truly been a blessing for us to know we get to honor each other in our relationship. We both have made bad decisions in the past due to lack of boundaries or to our failure to keep boundaries that were set. We decided early in our relationship that we didn't want to add to our testimony unnecessarily. That is, we didn't need to spin some wild or dramatic story about crossing and then keeping boundaries to make our testimony more appealing or "inspiring" to an audience. Instead, we believe that purity, through setting and keeping boundaries by the power of the Holy Spirit, represents just as effective of a testimony.

We will list our boundaries below, which include not holding hands—or as our accountability Pastor Melba Dunson calls it, "no hand-hunching." There's no such thing as extreme boundaries if they help keep you pure before God! Accordingly, when setting boundaries, it is important to take into consideration each other's weaknesses. Since holding hands was a struggle for Damien, I (Kenady) had to honor that request. Just because something is not a struggle for you doesn't mean it isn't for your partner. Make the necessary sacrifices so both people can come to the altar unadulterated.

Also, don't try to compete with other couples when placing boundaries. Don't turn your boundaries into decorated gates to show off to the world. Check your heart when setting a boundary: Is it pride-related and self-motivated? Or is it truly to keep you pure in order to honor and glorify God?

Your love languages may lead you to build boundaries. Damien's main love language is physical touch, hence not holding hands during our courtship and engagement season. If you know yourself, you should build boundaries to protect the relationship so you won't manipulate the other person to satisfy temporary pleasures and feelings.

We understand that a lot of couples have not encountered these foundational principles before. While other couples are already familiar with these concepts, they may never have taken the time to sit and actually write down their boundaries. We want to be transparent in this process by sharing what we did before we started getting really serious about our courtship. Over the course of two separate outings (dates, if you will), we wrote our boundaries and vision for our relationship. We signed these and sent them to our accountability couple, both Justin and Jasmine.

One significant disclaimer is that not all relationships are the same. Something that was a struggle for us may not be a struggle for your relationship, but regardless, your ultimate goal should be to stay pure and holy by any means necessary. Also of vital importance to our journey was prayerfully keeping the Holy Spirit involved along the way. God loves to be invited into our relationships—after all, He created relationships in the first place. One of the biggest things we see hindering godly, Christian relationships is that people don't consult God before making all of their relationship decisions. We operate out of the flesh and say, "God, now You bless it!" Brothers and sisters, it doesn't work like that. Romans 13:14 tells us, in part, to "make no provisions for the flesh, to gratify its desires" (ESV). Set boundaries to keep your flesh in check and in its rightful place!

Our Boundaries

1. Absolutely no sex!
2. No going over to each other's house.
3. Appropriate hugs only—like "side hugs," instead of pressing our bodies against each other for a prolonged period of time.
4. No kissing.
5. No inappropriate touching and petting.
6. No sexting.
7. No talking past 12:30 a.m. on the phone or FaceTime. (Note: On video chat, wear appropriate clothes before logging on.)
8. No holding hands. (However, we decided that it was okay to hold hands while praying.)

Again, don't feel like you have to compete with or imitate our boundaries. Work with your partner to create boundaries that are necessary and relevant for both of you in this current season. It's crucial to communicate honestly and pray over this list. Also, keep in mind that you may need to add new boundaries throughout your courtship journey in case there are any "close calls" or falls that occur along the way. Just be sure to start somewhere! Boundaries are so important to set at the beginning of a relationship because you are building your foundation on two important pillars: righteousness and holiness. When you have self-control, purity, and a heart to honor God and each other, you are setting yourself up for a successful and a significant marriage. You will be able to trust one another, remain pure, and continue to have self-control throughout your marriage. Temptation does not stop once you get married, and purity needs to be continued, so don't take boundaries lightly. If you are in a relationship, or even in a marriage, without explicit boundaries, it is not too late to set them up, either. Boundaries are for our benefit, no matter the season we're in.

What happens if you end up breaking up with your partner? Were these boundaries even worth it? Yes! You see, now you don't have to worry about carrying shame, guilt, or ungodly soul-ties to the next relationship, because you sought God and focused on keeping Him first, honoring Him and the other person in your relationship. Now you can thank that person and move on without unnecessary hurt or pain. Yes, it will hurt when you break up with somebody, but your soul will be in a healthy space if you have not crossed your boundaries. It is much easier to break up with someone with whom you haven't been physical and to whom you haven't given spousal privileges. Boundaries are for your benefit, regardless of where your courtship leads.

If you have broken boundaries repeatedly, and perhaps are currently living in sexual sin, but are serious about getting back on track and doing things the right way, we suggest you and your partner agree to take a step back from the relationship for a season (or in some cases, forever.) We encourage you to turn back to God and allow Him to set you free from lust. Then you can establish better boundaries in the future to help protect each other's walk as disciples. It's hard to try to break off lustful emotions and behavior together, with someone else who's dealing with the same issue. Seek accountability to help guide you in this walk to sexual purity. God might be calling you back into courtship with that person or to separate forever. No matter the outcome, the goal is to live a pure life that is fully submitted and glorifying to God.

#COMPLETELYMARRIED

Chapter 3:
Vision

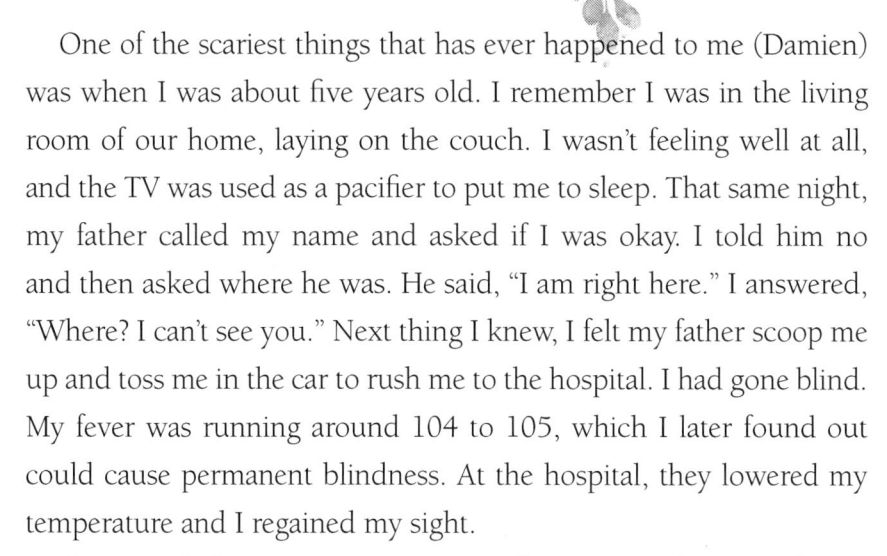

One of the scariest things that has ever happened to me (Damien) was when I was about five years old. I remember I was in the living room of our home, laying on the couch. I wasn't feeling well at all, and the TV was used as a pacifier to put me to sleep. That same night, my father called my name and asked if I was okay. I told him no and then asked where he was. He said, "I am right here." I answered, "Where? I can't see you." Next thing I knew, I felt my father scoop me up and toss me in the car to rush me to the hospital. I had gone blind. My fever was running around 104 to 105, which I later found out could cause permanent blindness. At the hospital, they lowered my temperature and I regained my sight.

Temporarily losing your vision is not fun. You are disoriented. You don't know where you are or where you are going. Losing a function in which you previously had so much confidence can leave you feeling helpless.

However, in relationships, some people seek a vision at first but then give up on pursuing it; in other words, they choose blindness. When this happens—which it does, far too often—it's heartbreaking. And this occurs not only in the world but also in the church. We talk about so many things that are pointless! We are attracted to the wrong things while remaining oblivious to what real godly fruit looks like.

Discovering Your Personal Vision

We love George Barna's definition for vision when it comes to ministry because your potential relationship with the opposite sex is for ministry purposes. Therefore, it needs to have a vision! A vision is "a clear mental image of a preferable future imparted by God to His chosen servants and is based upon an accurate understanding of God, self and circumstance."[5]

But here is the trick: How can you have a vision for your relationship if you don't have a personal vision for yourself? We try to rush into a relationship instead of rushing into the presence of God to figure out what we are here for and what His vision is for our lives. To start developing a process for finding your personal vision, and then a vision for your relationship, you should 1) spend time with God, 2) spend time with yourself alone, and 3) spend time with wise counsel.

1. Spending time with God helps you get to know God. This might involve a fast or reading His word. You will never be disappointed as a result of spending time with God, nor will you ever have to worry that you're spending too much time with Him.

2. Spending time with yourself is not a bad idea. Before jumping into a relationship or dating random people, treat yourself to a meal or go out for a movie. Celebrate this season of your life. Get to know who you are and your personality. See what gifts, skills, and abilities you have to offer and bring to the table with your next Kingdom partner. What things have you put yourself through, or has God allowed you to go through, to help someone else? Write these things down in a journal so you can pull them out at the appropriate time.

3. Spending time with wise counsel is something I (Damien) did a lot in my single years. I wanted people to encourage me and to point out faulty thought processes that could be detrimental to my future spouse. I thank God for the people I sought out and whom God brought into my life. They helped me out tremendously as I searched for my mate. My vision was a lot clearer when my counsel spoke into my life!

Vision Before "I Do"

We, Damien and Kenady, have talked about what the vision for relationships should be prior to getting married and came up with three principles that will serve as the basis for the rest of this chapter. Take to heart what we said earlier and understand what God's vision for your life is before rushing into a relationship. This is critical, as you don't want to get caught in the same cycles, dating the same type of people. So, what is your vision? Better yet, what is your objective? Before soldiers are deployed into battle, they receive their objectives. Before you enter your next relationship, consider and remember these three objectives: 1) **Kingdom** before family, 2) **purpose** before partner, and 3) **wholeness** before oneness. We believe that if you are not married yet and you start here, focusing on these three principles, you will establish a better foundation for your relationship.

Three "Values Azimuths"

Before we dive deeper into developing your vision for your next relationship, we want to touch briefly on your values. In June 2018, I (Damien) was driving for a popular rideshare company and picked up a courteous gentleman named Jim in Dunwoody, Georgia. As soon as he got into the back passenger seat, he said, "Damien, how are you?" I thought it was very polite of him to look up my name and acknowledge me. You might be surprised how few people acknowledge drivers.

We had a pleasant conversation, as he was interested in my coaching practice—how I walk alongside individuals in setting and achieving their goals. After I shared a bit, he offered a relevant analogy: "Damien," he said, "I was in the 82nd when I was in the war. We used to jump out of planes, but we didn't know where we were. We had our objective and plan of attack, but we never knew where we were going to land exactly. So we had to shoot an azimuth in three directions to see where we were. Then the compass would detect our location and we would start the objective."

At this point, you're probably asking, "What in the world is an azimuth?" My curiosity got the best of me, and I asked Mister Jim to spell out the word for me so I could write about it later. Webster defines *azimuth* as "an arc of the horizon measured between a fixed point (such as true north) and the vertical circle passing through the center of an object usually in astronomy and navigation clockwise from the north point through 360 degrees."[6] We now want to offer you three "values azimuths" that you can shoot within the first couple of conversations to see if your relationship is heading toward your true north, which is Christ. As our culture continues to move further and further from Christ, we must put our stakes in the ground as disciples of Christ. We must proclaim that we won't be like the rest of the world and there are certain things we cannot compromise because of our faith. Therefore, discuss these values before the vision is accepted or even written out—because they can also be deal-breakers and you don't want to waste your time or the time of the person you are trying to court. Values, as Tony Stoltzfus puts it, are the bedrock of behavior.[7] They define what is most important to us, form the framework we use for making decisions, and are the driving force behind our work and our passions.

Shot #1: Mutual respect. As we told you in the introduction of this book, I (Damien) was not having sex with Kenady, point blank. I respected her and her family too much, and she respected me to the point that we wouldn't even hold hands. Not every couple are that extreme, but because my main love language is physical touch, any physical contact gets me excited. I told Pastors Darius and Melba, our more mature accountability couple, after they questioned us about our handholding boundary, "The Holy Spirit can hold her hand. She'll be all right. I'll hold her hand at the altar." I was serious. Yes, it was tough, but it was what I had to do to stay pure. Another thing Kenady did well was 'check' me if I became too fleshly on FaceTime. If I grew too flirtatious, she would say, "Enmity," and hang up the FaceTime. All I would be left with were my feelings and a black iPhone screen staring back at me. She was protecting herself at all costs.

One day, I was meeting Kenady at the mall for one of our Saturday dates, and I phoned her because she was running late, which was unusual for her. When she answered, clearly she was not in her car, but I wanted to make sure. "Where are you?" I asked. "I am still getting ready, babe. I'm sorry," she responded. Two thoughts then rushed to the front of my mind. The first thought told me to get a bit upset and say, "Why did you tell me 2 o'clock if you weren't going to be ready?" The other thought said, "Kenady is going out tonight after church, to her class reunion, and so she is putting on makeup. She probably needs some more time."

Thankfully, I went with the second thought as I took the negative thought captive and said to myself, "How can I serve her?" So I asked her if she wanted me to stay in the car or go inside. She answered,

"Go inside. I don't want you to stay in the car waiting on me." I told her okay and that I'd see her soon. There you have it! I saved an argument by using respectful language. We respect each other by not talking negativity or talking down to each other. Besides being positive people, anyways, we recognize that our North Star is Christ, who is the Prince of Peace, so we are super-intentional about being positive even when we have the opportunity to say something slick or witty. We just don't tear each other down for no reason. When we do make a mistake, we try to rectify the incident, apologize, and move on quickly. After all, we have work to do in the Kingdom and don't have time to be immature and give offense or allow it to last for days.

Shot #2: Mutual purpose. At the time of writing this book, I (Damien) am a radio host, certified life coach, author, and speaker and doing ridesharing on the side. Kenady is currently enrolled in her dietetic internship as she seeks to become a registered dietitian. How is that the same purpose? Because purpose is bigger than jobs. So many couples seem to get this confused. We love bringing the kingdom of God wherever we are at the moment, ministering to our co-workers and encouraging them to live for God. We also serve together at church on the Pray and Care Team as we pray for the new members joining our church. We have talked about future plans to speak to different groups, whether they're churches or schools. We are not going in two opposite directions but in mutual directions.

The Latin prefix for two is *di-*. Be careful whom you start making plans with, and make sure you do not have two visions, because two visions lead to *division* and division can lead to *divorce*. This is why choosing a spouse is probably the second biggest decision after accepting Christ as your Savior.

Shot #3: Mutual growth. The mutual growth we are talking about is not just professional. Yes, it's good to have certificates and degrees to help you walk through some doors in the marketplace. However, more importantly than that, are you growing spiritually, individually and together? Are both of you saved? Do you attend church on a regular basis? Do you have a church home? Do you read and study the Bible? These are extremely important questions to ask yourselves early on. We knew where we both stood because we attended the same church. Establishing that you're equally yoked spiritually (2 Corinthians 6:14) is one of the smartest things you can do at the beginning of a relationship. Relationships can be tough enough without ignoring potential conflict in such a critical, foundational aspect of your life.

Of course, careers matter, too. Does your partner have aspirations to grow in their industry or field? This might mean growing in expertise and mastery of his or her current position or advancing to a more senior position. Regardless, it is attractive when a person wants to grow in his or her occupation.

Kingdom Before Family

Don't *solely* focus on the family. We're *not* criticizing the well-known ministry called Focus on the Family, but we're challenging the prevailing mindset of the generation of singles and young adults that I (Damien) have led over the years. Christian families nowadays can become complacent. We get up on Sundays, go to church, eat Sunday meals, and then go to sleep. We might do an outreach here or there, but it's only to check it off the list. We return home, and when the garage closes, that's the end of the outreach. We have become self-protective Christians instead of self-reflective disciples.

After my Roman trip, I saw how direly the gospel of Jesus Christ is still needed in the world today, and we can't get bored with sharing the gospel. No matter what platform we are on, everything should point to the gospel message! Kenady and I focused very early on the Kingdom, which drew us ever closer and fed our excitement about getting married. Yes, where we live is important, but sharing the gospel where we live is even more important. When Kenady and I were courting, I was not in the financial place I thought I should be, but spiritually, I knew that I was in a great place to push the Kingdom forward and seek to make disciples for Christ. I believed God would take care of the rest.

We know that your family should be your first ministry, but don't leave it as your only ministry. When you have a Kingdom mindset, as you are building a foundation for your family, you will continue to have that mindset and not disappear from Kingdom work. So, when you are looking for someone to build a family with, think about ways in which you can advance the Kingdom together. We implore you not to focus on the family to the exclusion of the Kingdom. Instead, strive to build a Kingdom family.

Purpose Before Partner

In today's society, there has been an overemphasis on relationships and marriage. We esteem marriage as if it's a reward and despise singleness as if it's some sort of punishment. The Word of God says in 1 Corinthians 7 that singleness and marriage are both a gift from God. There is nothing wrong with desiring marriage, but when we put all of our focus and effort into trying to get married, it becomes an *idol* and we can become *idle* in our growth as disciples of Jesus Christ. We can miss out on the purpose God has for us right now, before we encounter our partner.

Many people think that they have no purpose or value if they aren't in a relationship. Too often, people believe their sole purpose in life is to be married or that their purpose only starts after marriage. This is a lie straight from the enemy, which is causing us to be discontented and keeping us from being effective in our singleness. Figure out what God wants you to do right now, and be aware of and thankful for the many blessings all around you. Don't wait for your partner to start walking in purpose. It wasn't until Adam was already walking in purpose, tending to the garden of Eden (Genesis 2:15) and naming the animals God had created (Genesis 2:19) that Eve was brought to him. When Boaz found Ruth, she was working and walking in her purpose. So if you are a single and reading this, do not waste any more time sitting around waiting for your partner. God knows the desires of your heart, and in due time, that special person will come if it is God's will.

This subject is so near and dear to my heart because I (Kenady) struggled with not being married for so long. I envisioned myself being married at a young age of 22. It wasn't until I was fed up with failed relationships and situations, and was no longer searching for someone, that Damien came into my life. Quite frankly, I didn't even want a relationship at the time. I just wanted to be diligent in completing my dietetic internship and healing from past hurts. I stepped into that season of relationship with Damien once I no longer made relationships and marriage an idol. Our relationship was not an award for my well doing, but rather a blessing that I was finally ready to receive without sabotaging my relationship with God or destroying myself. God, in His undeserved love and mercy toward us, does not want us to bring disaster upon ourselves by building up idols in our lives. He is a jealous God and a loving Father who wants all of our heart and devotion above everything and everyone else.

Now, I'm not saying that as soon as you no longer think about relationships or marriage, God will immediately send your partner your way. It is in His will and His timing. Rather, I am encouraging you to fill your time with doing God's will and being in His presence so that you can be fulfilled regardless of your relationship status. In due time, you will be ready for your partner and will have something to bring to that relationship.

Wholeness Before Oneness

Have you ever heard someone say, "He completes me," or "She is my better half"? I know these sayings are often used romantically or as expressions of endearment, but if you think about it, they can also express a form of idolatry. These sayings represent a person, and place an expectation on that person, in terms meant for God alone. No spouse or person can ever complete us, only God. If a spouse were meant to complete us, what does that mean for people who are single, including those who never get married? Was Paul, being a single man, considered incomplete? Was Jesus lacking something because He was not married? Of course not! People don't complete us; it is the work of God in us, and God Himself, that does this.

Genesis 2:21–23 says:

> And the LORD God caused a deep sleep to fall on Adam, and he slept; and He took one of his ribs, and closed up the flesh in its place. Then the rib which the LORD God had taken from man He made into a woman, and He brought her to the man. And Adam said: "This is now bone of my bones and flesh of my flesh…" (NKJV)

Yes, God took a rib from Adam, but was Adam incomplete simply because he was missing a rib? Was Eve only worth the value of one rib in Adam's life? Of course not! You see, God *repaired* Adam when He closed him up, which bestowed healing and wholeness. Missing one rib was not a life-or-death situation. As Damien says, "he'll be all right" with one less rib. Then God formed Eve from the rib as a complete human being, which likewise bestowed wholeness and value. Eve wouldn't even have known she was taken from a man without someone telling her as much. She certainly didn't need any man to have worth, because her worth was in God. When we allow for God to do a work in our lives and in our hearts, then we can truly be healed from past hurts and feel value where before we felt worthless.

Adam had discernment and knew Eve was made from his flesh, which meant they had similar DNA. He knew they were compatible, or equally yoked, in a way that they weren't compatible with the animals. Accordingly, we need to seek *compatibility*, not *completion*, from our spouse. A husband and wife should be able to come together as two whole individuals to work in complete harmony and oneness to perform the purposes God has given them. This unity depicts the oneness of the Trinity as well as the unity of Christ and His bride, the church.

Notice that in the Bible, it does not say half a person and another half a person become one full person; it says two shall become one flesh. Two become one for purpose, not for completion. Those two should already be whole individuals. Granted, you and your spouse will have different strengths and weaknesses, and you both will be able to work with each other and sharpen each other. God can also use your spouse to continue the healing and pruning process, as His vessel, but your spouse will never be the Source.

So seek to be *whole* before you seek to be one. When the time is right, God will bring you both together to work in unity and oneness.

We never knew how important vision was until we wrote ours down during courtship. It is the underpinning of who we are and what type of relationship we desire to have. Most people may never see your vision, but they will see you. We pray that you take heed of the information in this chapter before you continue reading. Our desire is for you to have a strong foundation and better yet, a clear vision before you move on in any relationship. We have talked to countless couples who are courting, or even married, but don't have a unified vision. Avoiding these conversations in the beginning leads to unnecessary misunderstandings, conflict, strife, and hurt later on.

In the next chapter, we'll give you questions to spark your creativity and enhance your vision beyond your current cultural background. We are just getting started!

Part 2:
Courtship Journey

#COMPLETELYMARRIED

Chapter 4:
The Beginning Stages of Courtship

We will never forget April 8, 2018. On this date, I (Damien) asked Kenady to be my lady. I'll share my version of how it all went down, and then Kenady will add her perspective.

If you're a man reading this book, you might want to take some notes. And if you are a woman, fair warning: it's about to get mushy, so be prepared to "aww!" or "wooow!" as needed.

I'll be honest and reveal that I got a bit of help with what to do. I am *not* a romantic in the slightest, and I made sure I shared this with Kenady at the beginning of our friendship. I told her that romance is a muscle I have to be intentional at exercising because my natural preference is to just get to the point, get it over with, and go home—otherwise, I tend to overthink things. For this reason, I did solicit some input in planning for this particular day. I won't give up my source, in part because I may need more help in the future, but just know that the advice was perfect.

I was already fully confident that Kenady would say yes to courtship. She had been hinting that she wanted me to ask her to be my girl, but I never tipped my hand as to when or where. The day before, one of her small-group members actually called me and said she had talked about me *all* evening. He added that he had never seen a girl so happy before. (That's how we Nash boys do it.)

We had scheduled a get-together at Stone Mountain. I played this day as being an exercise and "getting to know each other more" date. After we met up at a parking lot, we embraced with a hug and started walking toward the base of the mountain. Then we stretched, took a quick bathroom break, and started our ascent.

As we walked and talked, one of the major topics that came up was vision. Significantly, I noticed that we shared some similar life-goals. The longer we continued our trek up the mountain, though, the more we refrained from spending our energy on conversation because we were both gassed. I even asked several times, "Okay, do you want to turn back?" She was empathetic in her responses but insisted, "No, let's keep going." I'd asked the question to see if I had found a ride-or-die partner—and I most definitely had.

We finally made it to the top of the mountain. I needed a breather and to prepare mentally, so I took another bathroom break. I returned to Kenady trying to figure out where I would present her with my card and handwritten note, but she took the lead and led me to the side of the mountain. While we were walking, I reached into my blue backpack, sliding my hand past my chilled water bottle and #CompletelySingle sweatshirt, and retrieved the card. As soon as she turned around, *bam!*—I surprised her by shoving the card into her personal space. "Aww!" she said while reaching into her bag to retrieve an origami personal note that she had made for me. Clearly, we'd been thinking along similar lines.

I pulled out my phone to capture her reaction while she read my note. I'll refrain from typing out the whole note here (since I'd like to keep my man card), but I can give you the gist. In the note, I declared that February 22, 2018, was probably the best day of my life because at 3:36 p.m., I'd decided to reach out to her again on DM. I also stated that mountains are tough to climb up alone, but with someone else it's that much easier. The note concluded by asking, "So will you walk together with me in courtship? Please give your answer at this time." On reading this, Kenady said "aww" again and tried to hug me, but I responded, "Nah, girl. Yes or no." Then she said yes (of course, after all that planning) after which I gave her the #CompletelySingle sweatshirt (which was the right size, by the way) and wristband, officially knighting her as #CompletelySingle and officially making her my lady.

So, how did I do?

Kenady's Notes

I (Kenady) know that this is the part you've been waiting for—though I must say, on the whole, Damien did a great job at telling our April 8, 2018, story. However, he failed to mention a few crucial details. As mentioned earlier, in our introduction on how we met, I was originally afraid to give Damien my number. After rededicating my life to Christ, I did not give out my number often because I just wasn't sure if I was ready to go there and take that step with anyone. This did not stop Damien from pursuing me or calling me (via Facebook audio).

A few weeks into our friendship and getting to know each other better, he joked about how he still didn't have my number. In response, being the goofball that I am, I decided to give him my number in pieces, starting with the area code. A few weeks later, he mentioned that his boys had been clowning on him for still not having my number. To make him feel better, I gave him my next three digits and told him six out of ten isn't bad. Realizing that my last four digits now held a special meaning, I decided I was going to wait until the perfect time to reveal them to him. I told my roommate and some of my friends what my plan was, and they were pumped about it. As the days went by, I started to feel bad about playing with him and not giving him my number, but I was impressed at his patience. He wasn't going to let a few digits stop him from getting to know me more!

As it happened, he planned a walk up Stone Mountain the very day that I intended to give him the rest of my phone number. I decided I would write him a sweet note, as well, and fold it the way I would back in my middle school days. I also bought him one of his favorite snacks of all times, animal crackers. When the day finally arrived and I met him at Stone Mountain, I was so excited to surprise him. Just one thing was standing in my way: the mountain. I thank God that it was not a typically hot day in Georgia. The cloud cover and breeze were definitely on our side. We made it to the top in record time, for me at least, with Damien being a great partner and encouraging me along the way.

As I took Damien to a secret spot on the mountain, he pulled out a card and handed it to me. In return, I gave him my handwritten note. Like Damien, I have decided not to disclose what was written in the note I wrote because I want to maintain my tough-gal image and not reveal my true sappy tendencies. But I'll tell you this: he was cheesing from ear to ear.

At the bottom of the note, I put the day's date: 4/8/18. In parenthesis, I wrote: "(this is not just today's date but also my last 4 digits of my phone number)." How crazy is that? Damien was shocked and in disbelief. The date he had planned to ask me into a courtship was the same as my last four digits, which he had waited for so patiently. You couldn't write a better story than that, could you? This is the epitome of waiting on God's perfect timing: before the foundation of the world, He had already written every detail.

Intentionality Is Key

Courtship is intentional. Our courtship was *very* intentional. Before we ever got together, I (Damien) fasted from one particular food item. I believe it's important to prepare yourself by fasting to train your body and develop more self-control. Kenady also read my book *#CompletelySingle* before we entered into courtship because we wanted to be on the same page. She still says I was scheming to get her to fall in love with me when I gave her a free copy of my book—and on some level, she might be right.

I don't really like using the word *dating*, even though many in the church use it. After I prayed about the meaning of *courtship*, as an alternative to the term *dating*, I believe I was given this healthy definition, a version of which I included in *#CompletelySingle*: courting is developing a relationship with the opposite sex to see if God is leading you to an external union for eternal purpose, without undermining your walk as a disciple of Jesus Christ.[8]

We decided to write this book because we have witnessed too many Christian couples who have relationships like the world. They have no purpose or intentionality, and nothing is getting done to further the kingdom of God. Another reason was to give us something to work on as teammates early in our relationship. We are a team, and having purpose kept our minds off of sinning together. If you don't have anything to devote your energy to, and help each other with, it just leaves you both with more time to think about sinning together before marriage. I personally wanted to eliminate every opportunity for that inside our courtship.

Now, we didn't work on the book during every outing—we did fun things, as well. But as I discuss in *#CompletelySingle*, a sense of purpose is key. In a relationship or marriage, be able to answer the question, "Why are we going where we are going?"

Purpose Project

We suggest praying that God gives you both a "purpose project" for the duration of your courtship. This can be a mutual project that's fun to complete, and it may start within the courtship but finish after marriage, like our book. We're not saying that it has to be as grand as writing an entire book together, but it should be something you agree upon, in which you're both genuinely invested—and above all, something that you finish together.

So, what are the specific benefits of having a purpose project?

Focus on intimacy. The intimacy to which we're referring is more with the Father than with each other. Yes, I (Damien) wanted to have a physical intimate relationship with Kenady, and that would come after "I do." However, I always want to be more in love with God and what He has for me to do. This means we were spending time studying, praying, and meditating on God's word so our book would reflect God's heart. Our intimacy with God grew deeper as a result. I also found during this process that I struggled less with lust when I thought more about completing the project. When we met up to write, I can honestly say, I mostly thought about finishing what we started. Sure, there were occasional moments when I fell—admiring Kenady eyes or noticing her body way too long, for which I repented—but my mind would then return to the project, and that's where it typically stayed. I wanted to live a life of purity and focus intentionally on my relationship with God, and Kenady knew this. My love for God, with purpose, needed to be the driving force throughout the whole relationship.

Purpose Project

We suggest praying that God gives you both a "purpose project" for the duration of your courtship. This can be a mutual project that's fun to complete, and it may start within the courtship but finish after marriage, like our book. We're not saying that it has to be as grand as writing an entire book together, but it should be something you agree upon, in which you're both genuinely invested—and above all, something that you finish together.

So, what are the specific benefits of having a purpose project?

Focus on intimacy. The intimacy to which we're referring is more with the Father than with each other. Yes, I (Damien) wanted to have a physical intimate relationship with Kenady, and that would come after "I do." However, I always want to be more in love with God and what He has for me to do. This means we were spending time studying, praying, and meditating on God's word so our book would reflect God's heart. Our intimacy with God grew deeper as a result. I also found during this process that I struggled less with lust when I thought more about completing the project. When we met up to write, I can honestly say, I mostly thought about finishing what we started. Sure, there were occasional moments when I fell—admiring Kenady eyes or noticing her body way too long, for which I repented—but my mind would then return to the project, and that's where it typically stayed. I wanted to live a life of purity and focus intentionally on my relationship with God, and Kenady knew this. My love for God, with purpose, needed to be the driving force throughout the whole relationship.

Intentionality Is Key

Courtship is intentional. Our courtship was *very* intentional. Before we ever got together, I (Damien) fasted from one particular food item. I believe it's important to prepare yourself by fasting to train your body and develop more self-control. Kenady also read my book *#CompletelySingle* before we entered into courtship because we wanted to be on the same page. She still says I was scheming to get her to fall in love with me when I gave her a free copy of my book—and on some level, she might be right.

I don't really like using the word *dating*, even though many in the church use it. After I prayed about the meaning of *courtship*, as an alternative to the term *dating*, I believe I was given this healthy definition, a version of which I included in *#CompletelySingle*: courting is developing a relationship with the opposite sex to see if God is leading you to an external union for eternal purpose, without undermining your walk as a disciple of Jesus Christ.[8]

We decided to write this book because we have witnessed too many Christian couples who have relationships like the world. They have no purpose or intentionality, and nothing is getting done to further the kingdom of God. Another reason was to give us something to work on as teammates early in our relationship. We are a team, and having purpose kept our minds off of sinning together. If you don't have anything to devote your energy to, and help each other with, it just leaves you both with more time to think about sinning together before marriage. I personally wanted to eliminate every opportunity for that inside our courtship.

Now, we didn't work on the book during every outing—we did fun things, as well. But as I discuss in *#CompletelySingle*, a sense of purpose is key. In a relationship or marriage, be able to answer the question, "Why are we going where we are going?"

Focus on strengths and weaknesses. As you work on your purpose project, you can gain a concrete, real-time picture of what each of you is good at and not so good at. Maybe your partner is great at generating a ton of ideas but isn't as effective at executing, or following through. Perhaps one of you is talented at strategy and branding but struggles at budgeting the project out. When you start this project in courtship, you'll have a leg up on your relationship before you start cooperating on projects in marriage. You will encounter a lot of surprises during marriage, but understanding each other's work ethic and habits can help you eliminate heated discussions and arguments.

Focus on Kingdom work. Yes, you can have fun, but when it comes to Kingdom work and your project, you must sacrifice. This means you might see your friends and families less frequently. When we join together as husband and wife, the Bible says, we leave our own fathers and mothers and cling to each other (Genesis 2:24). We've seen a lot of couples who still have their umbilical cord attached even after marriage, which puts a strain on the new couple's relationship. One reason could be that they didn't have the purpose talk before they got married and really understood the scripture above. But we have prayed that will not be your relationship.

Even more importantly, you might see your friends and families less often because you want to be found where God has called you to work. Jesus said clearly, in Luke 14:26–27, "If anyone comes to me and does not hate his own father and mother and wife and children and brothers and sisters, yes, and even his own life, he cannot be my disciple. Whoever does not bear his own cross and come after me cannot be my disciple" (ESV). Then in verse 33, He concluded, "So therefore, any one of you who does not renounce all that he has cannot be my disciple" (ESV).

Whenever God establishes a purpose for someone, we see in the Bible, the person can be found working:

- Adam was found working in the Garden. (Genesis 2:19)
- Elisha was found working in the field. (1 Kings 19:19)
- Ruth was found working in Boaz's field. (Ruth 2:5–7)
- David was found working tending sheep. (1 Samuel 16:11–13)
- Matthew was found working by collecting taxes. (Matthew 9:9–13)

Our relationships can't be all about adventure and entertainment, because He is still looking for sacrificial individuals who will forfeit fun for future.

Getting to Know Each Other

Before and after you enter into courtship, you should spend a lot of time getting to know each other. In #*CompletelySingle*, we talked about the term *yada*, which means "to know."⁹ One of the biggest mistakes a couple can make early on, which is prevalent even among Christians, is thinking they need to have sex to get to know each other. That is a false narrative, and in future chapters, we will talk extensively about how God created us and the order of sex.

Don't think you have to live with somebody—the usual term today is "shacking up"—to get to know them before marriage, either. At worst, this leads to sexual sin, but even with the best intentions, it places unhealthy pressure on the relationship.

In this section, we will provide you with some of the questions we asked each other, which solidified that we were on the same page. We came up with our own questions, though we also used Heather and Cornelius Lindsey's book *So You Want to Be Married* as a reference guide to get to know each other on a deeper level. These questions are meant to dive deep into important aspects of life, but remember: they're only as useful as your willingness to share truthfully with each other about who you are behind closed doors.

Spiritual
- What are your spiritual beliefs?
- How and when did you come to the knowledge of Christ?
- How's your spiritual walk with Christ? How is your prayer life? What are your habits when it comes to spending time in the Word (Reading/Studying the Bible)?
- What has God spoken to you about lately?
- What are your spiritual gifts?

Finances
- What are your thoughts on giving to the poor/needy, tithing, and giving offerings?
- How much debt do you have? Do you know how to budget?
- Do you like to spend a lot of money, or do you like to save money?
- How do you want to handle finances in marriage?
- Do you have investments, life insurance, or retirement plans?

Family
- Where do you want to live?
- Do you have any kids? How many kids do you want to have?
- How do you plan to discipline your kids?
- Describe your intended family dynamics.
- How's your relationship with your relatives (e.g., parents, siblings, extended family)?
- Do you have/want pets?

Cleanliness
- What are your standards for personal hygiene?
- What are some pet peeves you have regarding cleanliness?
- How clean do you keep your house?
- How clean do you keep your car?
- How often do you do laundry?

Recreation
- What do you like to do for fun?
- What types of music do you listen to?
- What types of movies do you like to watch?
- How often do you eat out or enjoy entertainment (e.g., sporting events, movies, concerts)?
- How often do you want to hang out with your friends?

Future
- What do you see or feel that God is calling you to do?
What is your purpose, or your "why"?
- What are your career goals?
- Do you want to further your education?
- When do you want to retire?
- Describe your dream wedding and honeymoon.

Past

- Describe your past relationships.
- What struggles (vices) have you dealt with in the past or are you dealing with now?
- How were your childhood and your relationship with your parents growing up? What frustrates you?
- What generational curses/strongholds do you have in your family? What concerns arise from your family medical history?
- Have you experienced any traumatic events in the past that you can share? If so, what?

Miscellaneous

- Are you currently in a relationship or seeing somebody?
- How do you process pain? Is it easy or hard for you to forgive?
- Describe something you've done that you have regretted.
- Describe your best friend.
- If you were to inherit a million dollars, what would do with it?
- Do you have an accountability partner?

#COMPLETELYMARRIED

Chapter 5:
Maintaining Your Other Relationships

Have you ever entered a romantic relationship and, as a result, neglected all of your other relationships? You know, the people you did life with before you got boo'd up. We're not talking about old flings but friends and family. Or maybe you have been on the other side: your friend or relative neglected you after finding a new love interest. We encourage you to maintain a life with friends outside of your courtship. No, things probably won't be exactly the same, and you won't get to hang out with them like before as you grow deeper into courtship, but don't completely drop all of your other friends and family. You don't want to be so consumed with the person you're courting that he or she becomes an idol. And if you end up breaking off the courtship, you don't want to find yourself utterly devastated and alone because you no longer have that person consuming all of your time and energy.

It's unloving to subject friends and family to a vicious cycle of picking up and cutting off whenever your relationship status changes, but it's also unwise, because they are vital in courtship. They can be an excellent support system. They are able to see things you can't and can help hold you accountable, pray for you, and sharpen you. Quite frankly, we need friends in this journey called life. Group outings can enhance your growth as a couple as well as help you keep boundaries and not fall into sexual sin or any other sins. It's also healthy to maintain separate time with your girls (for the ladies) and with your fellas (for the guys) in both courtship and marriage. Just make sure you are hanging out with the right crowd, who want the best for you and your relationship—family and friends who will respect your significant other and speak life over your relationship, not death out of jealousy.

Flock Together

About every two weeks, unless it was the dead of winter, I (Damien) would wash my car. Like I mentioned before, I was driving Rideshare and believed it was important to keep my car decent for those who might grace my back or front seats. One spring day, I decided to get a head start on the heat and humidity in Georgia and wash my car in the morning.

Unlike Kenady, I lived out near the country, where some of your pets are bound to be wildlife. For instance, over the previous couple of weeks, we'd had a young deer come visit us around the same time at night before the sunset. I wanted to be the first in my family to feed a wild deer, but the deer wasn't having it. It continued to run away when I tried to feed it a sweet potato. Other animals that frequently congregated around our house included cats and wild birds.

On this particular morning, I had already vacuumed my car and was halfway through spraying it down with the blue water-hose when I saw a giant shadow glide effortlessly across my front yard and then over the house. When I looked up, I saw a huge black bird with silver feathers on both wings. Glancing over the house, I noticed a similar bird. They were vultures. Now, whenever you see vultures around, you know there is something dead nearby. As more vultures began their morning flying exercises overhead, I became a bit unsettled, asking myself, "I am not the dead thing, am I?" Though I went back to washing my car, I cautiously took a peek into the partly cloudy blue sky every four to five minutes. At the pinnacle of their party, more than fifteen vultures were flying together, several hundred feet in the air.

You've heard the adage that "birds of a feather flock together." Our question to you is: What type of birds are you flying with? Vultures, also known as buzzards, are not typically anyone's favorite bird because they are always feasting on dead things.

Take a look at your current circle. Do you have people in your life who talk about dead things, listen to dead things, and are always flying up and down emotionally? One of the things that brought Kenady peace and minimized her worry was whenever I told her I was going out with the fellas. In our current culture, this would serve as a red flag in the minds of many women, warning of possible flirtation with infidelity or other sinful behavior. Why doesn't Kenady react this way? Simply because the crew I fly with are not carrion-eating vultures; they are eagles. If the person with whom you're in a relationship has started trippin', so to speak, maybe it's because your crew has a vulture mentality. By contrast, my crew is not trying to sleep with different women or partying in bars and clubs. My friends, some of whom have become my accountability, are faithful men of

God. They don't talk about cheating on their wives or purposely lying to their current courtship partners. They live for God, and they have a purpose.

We encourage you, ladies and gentlemen alike, to establish a mindset of surrounding yourself intentionally with wholesome individuals. The Bible is clear on this. Proverbs 13:20 says, "Walk with the wise and become wise; associate with fools and get in trouble" (NLT). You don't want your significant other to be concerned about whom you hang out with, or about your character being tainted. You want the person you're courting to be at ease when you are out with friends.

So ask yourself: "Who am I flying with?"

Covenant Relationships

Great blessings can be attached to flocking with the right crowd, especially in the context of covenant relationships. We will explain the different types of covenant principles in more detail in Chapter 10, but simply put, a covenant is a covering. In the Old Testament, entering into a covenant involved blood. Usually, an animal was offered up to seal the covenant. Then, in the New Testament, Jesus bled on the cross to be our covering, which established a new covenant with His children.

Biblically, a covenant is a bond, agreement, or oath made between God and His people, in which certain stipulations had to be upheld by the people. When the stipulation was met, there was always a blessing attached.

One of the stories that illuminates our understanding of a covenant is found in 2 Samuel 6. King David was traveling with the Ark of the Covenant to Jerusalem. During the journey, Uzzah, one of the sons of Abinadab, tried to prevent the Ark from falling after the oxen stumbled. As a result, he touched the Ark, which God did not permit. Uzzah died instantly. After seeing this, King David was terrified of the Ark. Instead of bringing it to Jerusalem, he brought it to the house of Obed-Edom the Gittite. The story continues in 2 Samuel 6:11–12:

> The ark of the LORD remained in the house of Obed-Edom the Gittite for three months, and the LORD blessed him and his entire household. Now King David was told, "The LORD has blessed the household of Obed-Edom and everything he has, because of the ark of God." So David went to bring up the ark of God from the house of Obed-Edom to the City of David with rejoicing. (NIV)

In this passage, we see that Obed-Edom and his household were blessed because the Ark of the Lord, also known as the Ark of the Covenant, was there—and not just for one day, but for three whole months. Imagine being blessed for three months! By contrast, David's blessing was delayed for three months due to fear, as he postponed bringing the Ark to Jerusalem. In the covenant relationship of God with David and the Israelites, being in His presence—in obedience—brought blessing.

Pay attention to the relationships you are in this season. While some relationships aren't worth the dysfunction, the hurt, and the lack of blessing, you can be blessed by intentionally developing covenant relationships. That's why small groups and biblical community are so important. The blessings can come in various forms, one being wisdom. For instance, it's a blessing to be around friends who are in healthy courtship or marriages, because they can give you advice on what to do and what not to do. You will also get a front-row seat to observe how to do relationships God's way, as well as the benefits that come from submission and obedience.

If the enemy can't get you isolated or in a toxic relationship, he will try to surround you with friends who are not totally surrendered to God, and who are themselves in toxic relationships, so that they can influence the way you do relationships. You might think, "Well, if so and so is doing it and they call themselves a Christian, I guess I can do it, too." These friends might also give you bad advice regarding your relationship: "Girl, sleep with your man, it's not going to kill you. God knows your heart." "You don't have to do all that, it's not that serious." "Your boundaries are too strict." This is all unredeemed advice that you do not want to heed, but when your flesh is weak, you might give in to such counsel.

That is why you need to be surrounded by people who are doing it God's way—so they can hold you accountable. You want friends to say, "Girl, why are you over at your man's house late at night? Aren't y'all trying to stay pure? I know the struggle is real. I've been there. But don't give up. It'll be so worth it. Let's pray together." Or, "Bro, leave that girl alone. She is not acting like a woman who is ready to live pure." We truly believe our lives are blessed and filled with supernatural peace because of the people we have around us. We were able to do this purity walk by the grace of God, yes, but also because we were not alone. We know several people in our lives who have done it and are doing it, which gave us comfort that we could do it, too. Though this approach is not popular, you are not the only one following God's prescription for relationships. Find like-minded individuals and couples and be in covenant relationship with them.

If you are single, we encourage you to surround yourself with married as well as single people. Singles ministries are a blessing, but covenant relationships with those who aren't single are also important. If you want to own a business, you hang out with business-minded people. If you want to launch a singing career, you are not going to hang out with plumbers or electricians 24/7—you'll surround yourself with producers, music executives, and others in the industry. You should apply the same mentality when it comes to establishing godly relationships. Just because you're #CompletelySingle doesn't mean you have to be around singles all the time. There needs to be a balance. As you start preparing your heart for the next season of your life, it's good to see godly married couples interact with each other and their children. No, you don't covet their relationships, but you do take notes. This is especially crucial if you come from a broken home and didn't see a godly, loving marriage in action.

And of course, these covenant relationships are mutually beneficial: you can be a blessing to the people you hang around with, just as much as you receive blessings through them. That's the beauty of covenant.

#COMPLETELYMARRIED

Chapter 6:
The Courtship Journey Continues— No Plan B

If you have a fear of failing, or of plans not working out like you think they're supposed to, you'll naturally want to have other plans to fall back on—a Plan B or C (or Z, depending on what type of person you are). Though it's not always bad to have a backup plan, when courting God's way there should *be no Plan B*. No Plan B means that you are saying goodbye to every other option out there and removing all ties to exes. One problem in our culture is that too many people accept looking at other women or men, in an interested or lustful way, before and after marriage. It's common to date multiple people at a time or to have other people lined up as backup plans or rebounds if the current relationship does not work out. If you have this kind of mindset, your relationships will always have shaky foundations. Most likely, you will struggle with commitment and faithfulness, looking for scapegoats and void-fillers at the first sign of conflict or trouble.

Too many of us approach relationships with this "don't put all your eggs in one basket" mentality. We want to offer you a different relationship paradigm: only carry one basket, and carry only one egg in it so you can focus on nurturing and protecting that single egg. If your egg cracks, you can go back to God to restore and heal that one egg, and He will show you if and when it is time to attempt to put the egg in a different basket. Having too many options results in divided attention and lack of commitment. Our relationship with God should be the same way. We should only bet on Him and not on anything or anyone else. He wants us to be all in or all out, not lukewarm with one foot in and one foot out "just in case it doesn't work."

When you're in a courtship that will hopefully end in marriage, you want to have a vision for commitment and covenant. Don't have your heart set on it, because you are not married yet, but establish a solid foundation with the right mindset: "I'm putting my one egg in this one basket. There's no one else I am currently interested in potentially marrying apart from you." You shouldn't live in fear or timidity. Yes, maintain your boundaries and proper pacing as God leads you, but don't hold on to other possibilities or leave windows open "just in case."

When the Past Comes Back

We know many of you can relate when we say that the past likes to try to pop back into your life—usually, into your phone—when you are in a committed relationship. Thank God for the "block" button! Unfortunately, though, this happened to me (Damien) while I was courting Kenady. Once, I received an especially heinous text message from somebody from my past. Shocked and appalled, I quickly forwarded it to Kenady because we were building an open door policy in our relationship. "Open door" means I don't intentionally try to hide anything from Kenady and she has full access to my phone, with reasonable exceptions for situations like surprises I'm planning for her. I won't share what this other young lady sent to me, because those details aren't necessary or constructive to relate, but she continued the onslaught. All I could do was shake my head. My brother had warned me, several months before I met Kenady, that before the right person comes along, a counterfeit will appear in your life—like a decoy. Those texts from the past showed that I had made the right decision in choosing Kenady.

So, what did I do? I let my accountability know what was going on and asked for advice. They thought someone had hacked the young lady's phone because the messages were so unbelievable. One of my spiritual mothers was afraid for my safety, and deep down, I was too. I decided to take the radical step of changing my number. Now, I know a lot of people. When I told my mother that I was changing my number, she pointed out that there were a lot of people who would not be able to get in touch with me. I told my mom I was willing to miss out on business opportunities and sacrifice other connections for Kenady. Within two days, I'd changed my number.

You can talk all day long about having no Plan B, but what ultimately counts is showing commitment in your actions. Nobody was going to get in the way of our relationship because I knew Kenady was the one. What about you? What are you willing to sacrifice for your significant other? Are you willing to close your social media accounts, change your email address, or get a new phone number? Those sorts of actions, when called for, will show your level of commitment not only to your boyfriend or girlfriend, fiancé or fiancée, or spouse, but also to God, who is the most important relationship any of us has.

Uncontrollables

Unexpected events can happen in any relationship. They can happen before marriage and will happen in marriage, so be prepared. In school, I (Damien) remember taking a marketing course in grad school and learning about several uncontrollables that affect marketing strategy: political, economic, weather, and competitors. I would add to this uncontrollable list that we must prepare for death. None of us knows the day or the hour when our name will be called or when a person close to us will leave this earth. However, we need to prepare our souls for these types of events because they will happen.

Even as we were writing this book, my father, Rev. John Al Nash, passed away. He had battled cancer for two and a half years. It was not tragic, but it was painful. As a couple, you get to be there for each other, but you will also learn a lot from the other person's faith. One word of advice: people respond differently to death. My twin brother lost his appetite when our father died; he didn't leave the house, and all he wanted to do was sleep. Such reactions are okay for a little while, but you should continue to provide comfort and support for the individual. Don't leave them alone for long periods of time. We had friends take my brother out so he would not be isolated with his own thoughts for too long.

For me (Damien), it was more about reflection than grief, but there were moments of intense sadness. In those cases, I tried to remember the good times and worship the Lord so my sadness wouldn't spiral into deep depression. Each of us has an opportunity, even if we do not feel like it, to worship the Lord through our pain and hurt. It's sometimes tough to remember in the moment, but James 1:2–4 (ESV) encourages us to "count it all joy" when we face trials.

For me (Kenady), it was a struggling season as well. I was dealing with sadness for Damien and his family and not being able to get to know my future husband's father like I'd always dreamed. However, he impacted my life greatly in the two precious moments I had to interact with him. I was grateful for those opportunities and will cherish them forever.

Despite being a person who likes to help and comfort people, I didn't know how to help Damien. I felt like I couldn't do anything specific for him—I could only be there for him. It is important to serve the person you're with, who is grieving in their "grief language," whatever that looks like. Some people like time alone, while others don't want to be alone. Some people want to talk, while others want to be quiet and not say a word. These preferences might change during different seasons or circumstances, so the best way to learn your partner's needs is by communicating openly on the subject.

Don't put pressure on yourself to cheer your partner up or fix their grief. When dealing with something like death, sometimes the most you can do is nothing. Allow God to do what only He can do. Be there for the other person in whatever way they want, not necessarily in the way you would want if your situations were reversed, as you continue to pray for comfort and seek guidance from God. During such a season, it is also important to extend greater grace and not take anything personally, whether it's your partner's emotional rollercoaster or simply not spending as much time together (if you are not married yet) for a while. Don't get offended. Just pray, love, and serve the other person through.

We also recommend that you familiarize yourself with the six (some sources say five to seven) levels of grief. I learned them as *shock, denial, anger, bargaining, depression,* and *acceptance.* When grieving, communicate with your partner from time to time about which level you think you may be at. If your partner is grieving and wants space, by all means, try to honor this request, but remember that emotionally healthy individuals also need biblical community to process the death of someone close.

Conflict

Being a son of a marriage counselor, I (Damien) have seen a lot of couples walk in and out of the door with fake smiles on their faces. After all, most people get counseling when things are not going so well. A better mindset would be to get counseling, or have accountability, to prevent things from getting 'too' bad in the first place. Though we never heard the intimate details about each couple, of course, we became aware of some of the issues that couples argue about, such as lack of communication, money, infidelity, and social media. Yes, social media has crept in to become one of the biggest distractions and disruptions in marriages. For instance, old flames are messaging people who are already married, creating drama and leading to major conflict in the home.

When conflict arises, do you have a way to deal with it successfully? A couple of years ago, I wrote a well-received piece on this topic. Here are the key points:

1. *Pray to the Holy Spirit.* Ask the Holy Spirit for strength, peace, and unity. Also, seek the Spirit for guidance, wisdom, and knowledge on how to handle situations. If the Holy Spirit knows all, why not ask Him?

2. *Seek to know all the information.* Make sure you gather all relevant information—and accurate information—before you start placing blame. Maybe the conflict is a result of a cultural misunderstanding. Maybe you misread the situation initially and will discover that you were, in fact, in the wrong. Whatever the case, it's important to become knowledgeable before you respond further.

3. ***Seize the initiative.*** Remember God in the garden with Adam and Eve after they had disobeyed Him? Instead of being bitter with His creation, He asked, "Where are you?"—seeking reconciliation and taking the first steps to find them. Likewise, be intentional to repair your relationship, even if you weren't in the wrong. (Personally, this is the one that I struggle with most.)

4. ***Position yourself as friend, not foe.*** Humble yourself and ask if the other person is ready to speak. If not, respectfully wait for a more suitable time. You don't want to come off as hostile or demanding.

5. ***Ask clarifying questions and listen to what is said.***
Make sure you are directing your questions to seek understanding, not just trying to be understood. Also, have mercy. Empathize with the other person, who might have reacted out of a place of pain—maybe a place familiar to you.

6. ***Seek a win-win outcome.*** Your goal is to solve a problem, not to win a fight. Either forgive the person at fault or repent for your own wrongdoing—maybe both, depending on the situation. As a Christian, you are to concern yourself with representing what is just, right, and true, which is the very foundation of the throne of God. In short, it's about righteousness, not proving you were right.

7. ***Sometimes conflict happens when you are trying to rout bad behavior.*** Yes, this might result in tense yet necessary conversations, but you should not tolerate bad behavior. That said, seek to have the spiritual fruit of kindness in the situation because after all, it's God's kindness that leads us to repentance.

I hope these seven principles bless you as they have blessed us. Whether at work, school, home, or church, offense will find you. It's how we handle disagreements that bring us the most freedom and the most glory to God. Ultimately, try to let go of offenses and conflicts quickly—remembering that by next week, today's conflict probably won't even matter.

Fighting Together, Not Each Other

We believe the foundation and framework for marriage start way before "I do." They begin when you are young. It's beneficial to be around examples of married couples from an early age, but of course, many people haven't had that opportunity. In writing this book, we hope to be part of the solution to the widespread lack of firsthand experience observing healthy marriages.

It baffles us to see so many people accepting crazy, messy relationships. You heard it from us: messy is not normal. Your relationship does not have to be drama-filled. If you're not already married, you can make a decision today to separate from a relationship that's filled with anger, cheating, or abuse. If possible, agree to take time apart to seek the healing you need to have a healthy relationship God's way. Relationships are designed to make us better. If you are dying inside or becoming a worse person, it is a clear sign that this might not be the right relationship for you.

If you are married, it's your responsibility to get help immediately, whether it be counselors, coaches, or therapists. You should be plugged into a church where resources and contacts are available to help you stay close to God. God hates divorce, so it's time to recalibrate and figure out how you two can rebuild a strong foundation of trust and accountability. With His help, you've got this! However it will take work from two people who are willing to fight together, not each other.

Stalemate

What does chess have to do with relationships? "Stalemate" is a term used when neither side can gain further advantage, meaning there is no winner or loser. A relationship can also have a stalemate. Now, we're not talking about having an argument with your spouse or significant other. Rather, you might *be* the stalemate—the mate who has become stale.

When I (Damien) surprised Kenady at work with a gift for Valentine's Day, one of the workers asked me to call her husband because "he needs lessons from you." It surprised me that the simple (albeit kind and romantic) act of bringing a gift to Kenady would prompt such a reaction. As I was meditating on this, I realized that from time to time, as couples, we tend not only to take our loved ones for granted but also—and even more seriously—leave out the help of the Holy Spirit. The Holy Spirit is not called the Helper for no reason!

If you want to know the secret to why Kenady is so blown away when I do things for her, it's because I am literally trying to involve the Holy Spirit in speaking her love languages to her. Have I done this every single time? Nope! But when I have paused and meditated, and experienced peace about undertaking particular actions, I've hit it out the park. The Spirit wants to be involved, and you will not fail with His advice. So this is my challenge for all of us—men and women alike, me included. No matter if it's gift giving, words of affirmation, physical touch, quality time, or acts of service, even something as simple as preparing food, invite the Holy Spirit in the mix.

You are doing a disservice to your fiancé (fiancée), courting/dating partner or spouse if you listen without truly hearing them. It's likewise doing a disservice when you wait until the last minute to prepare for a date that's been on the calendar for weeks, even months. The Holy Spirit wants to walk with you and help you prepare for special occasions. He wants you to meditate on what's been said so He can help you come up with a game plan to pursue your mate.

Listen, it's not ultimately about what gift you give or whether you receive anything in return. Who cares? That's not the point. If you are both thinking and caring about the other person involved, you'll learn their love language(s) and your hearts will draw ever closer together. These moments are certainly not for manipulation purposes—you give to give, and that's it. In turn, allow your partner to express his or her love according to God's leading, as appropriate for the level or stage of the relationship. We have seen amazing, supernatural results when we follow His guidance in these matters. In this way, instead of becoming stale mates, you can maintain the freshness of your relationship like it was in the beginning, when you first started courting.

Chapter 7:
Transitions—From Courting to Engaged

Within the first couple of weeks of our relationship, I (Damien) knew Kenady was the one. I was committed. I had an overall peace and confirmation regarding this within my circle of friends as well. One afternoon, we went to the mall and had her ring finger sized. Incidentally, in the process, we discovered that men's rings in the majority of the big chain stores don't get any respect. Kenady and I called the section in one store the "Rosa Park men's collection" because it was stuck all the way in the back corner.

By contrast, there was no shortage of options for women, but I noticed Kenady continuing to pick up a particular ring. Fellas, it's important to see what your lady is leaning toward. Don't be shy about taking pictures and asking lots of questions. Some women don't want expensive rings. They might want a stone. Regardless, you are here to serve her—and to be fiscally responsible. One goal I had—and achieved—was to start our marriage without "adding extra" debt. Ladies, you don't want the man to try to buy your love. You should never pressure your future spouse out of his current budget to impress people. Trust us, they will stop asking to see the ring after a few weeks. If the "two to three times your salary" rule is not an option, don't try to make it one. This is your relationship, and you have to answer to God on Judgment Day regarding how you handled the resources He entrusted to you. Yes, take it that seriously!

I didn't like the rings in the commercial retail stores I visited, so I went to AmericasMart in Atlanta. My friend, who used his business license to grant me access, took me to a wholesale ring shop called Danielle Diamond & Co. Since I knew my budget, I did not waste any time or try to play any games. Kenady wanted a rose gold double-halo cushion-cut diamond ring, so that's what I picked out. I negotiated with the owner and went on a three-month plan to pay it off.

The Proposal

The day I picked up the ring was the day they gave my father only two weeks to live. The week he died was a blur. But at the same time, I knew I needed to ask Kenady's father for his permission to marry his daughter. I was not scared or nervous about this, but with my father's decline and passing, there was a lot happening in a short time.

The funeral was on a Saturday. On the following Tuesday, I was awakened by the Spirit of the Lord, who said, "Ask him today." That caught me off guard because my initial plan had been to wait a couple more days, until that Friday. I asked God in prayer, "Is this just me, or is it really You?" Three times that morning, He confirmed it to me through prayer, with the impression growing stronger every time I prayed, so I had peace about this change of plans.

On the way to work on Tuesday, I picked up the phone and called Kenady's father. After we exchanged greetings, I got straight to the point. I told Mr. Pitts, "I believe your daughter is my wife, and I am asking for your blessing for her hand in marriage. You can pray about it if you want."

He responded, "I don't need to pray about it Damien. My answer is yes!" Then he added, "My spirit bears witness that you are a man of God." Boy, was I excited and relieved! I know his response would have made my father proud.

Now it was time to prepare for the proposal. One thing I did not do, but should have, was notify my aunt about the proposal. Thanksgiving dinner was going to be held at her house in 2018, but I only discussed my plan with her daughter, who I knew would help me with the proposal. That was a mistake, and we have to be accountable for our actions, especially as a disciple of Christ. After recognizing this error, I talked it over with my aunt, who hugged it out with me as family should.

As for the proposal plan itself, my idea was simple. Because my family is so big, we do Secret Santa for Christmas every year. On Thanksgiving, we draw the names, and I wanted Kenady involved this year. After my cousin brought the bag of names around to several family members, she would then sneak into the kitchen and switch it out for a bag of folded slips of paper that said, "Will You Marry Me?" If you go to YouTube and search for #PittsStoptoNash, you can see what happened next.

Don't Rush to the Altar

It's important during the engagement period not to rush anything. Our accountability advised us to enjoy this season and smell the roses. After the proposal, we decided to take a week just to enjoy being engaged, without talking about any wedding plans. We used this time to reflect individually, think about our finances, and pray to God for guidance on how long our engagement should be. It's easy to get ahead of yourself in the midst of all the excitement and speed through the process. Slow down, enjoy the moment, and be led by God.

Though we originally wanted to get married within a few months, we discovered during our reflection time—and once we met the following weekend to begin wedding plans—that God was telling us to wait. I (Kenady) had a dream that Damien was proposing and the diamond kept falling off. He attempted to glue it back together multiple times, but the glue was not finished drying yet. For his part, Damien found confirmation through prayer that we needed to slow down. We had an overwhelming peace about this, and it strengthened us, too, to know that we both had heard the same thing from God. We set a date accordingly.

That said, we encourage you to set a date, whenever that might be, so you can maintain a healthy vision for your relationship. You don't want to be lackadaisical and let years of engagement pass by. Remember, everything about courtship is intentional, so don't leave any room for confusion, wasted time or even temptation. Nor should you let external constraints, like a lease ending soon, dictate when you get married. Always seek counsel from God and your accountability.

What They Won't Tell You

How blessed we were to have accountability in Justin and Jasmine Hart! Their godly wisdom, which is too often absent from ministries and relationships within the church today—a reality God is motivating us to change—has propelled and inspired us in our relationship.

We Are Not One Yet

There is a transitional period, generally right before and during engagement, when you have to go deeper and have more adult conversations together and with your accountability. If you need godly counsel on a particular situation during this period, don't hesitate to come together and ask your accountability before making tough decisions. During our transition, we sought a godly perspective for a question pertaining to Kenady's living situation.

At the time, Kenady's lease was about to end, and she was not sure where she would stay prior to us getting married. She did not want to renew her lease for another year and set herself up for the hassle of finding someone to take over her lease—or having to pay to break her lease—once we got married. On the other hand, I (Damien) lived in a house with my twin brother and some other men, so I was not confined to a specific timeframe due to a lease agreement. We were thinking of different options for Kenady to transition as we planned ahead, including the possibility of her living with a couple from the church for a few weeks, or that of her renting an apartment where we would eventually live together, after marriage.

We were advised by our accountability couple that if we went with the apartment route, we should find a place with which we both felt comfortable but, ultimately, a place that Kenady could afford and would lease in her name only until we said, "I do." The key word is *afford*. Because Kenady was going to be the only one living in it for a few months, it would be wise and responsible for her to rent a place that she could manage on her own. Since we were not yet one, we shouldn't act as if we were.

We read a Bloomberg article about cohabitation trends among the younger generations. The article said, "Many poorer and less educated Americans are opting not to get married at all. They're living together, and often raising kids together, but deciding not to tie the knot. And studies have shown these cohabiting relationships are less stable than they used to be."[10]

It seems that many individuals are living outside their means, living together to save money, and avoiding the involvement of community—let alone God—in major life decisions regarding family formation. The results of this selfish behavior include perpetuation of the cycle as children grow up thinking it's okay for their parents to stay together without being married. By contrast, cohabitation was not even a question for us.

If you currently find yourself in a cohabitation situation, we urge you to look to God for conviction—with the understanding that this doesn't mean condemnation. Unlike the many members of the body of Christ who stay silent on such matters, in order not to offend, we want to point you back to the cross, lovingly. Your next step is to repent, which means to turn from the way you've chosen to live and embrace Christ's way of doing things. This may be tough to hear, but we encourage you to move out of your shared living space and get separate places. If children are involved, explain your decision to them based as one of living for the Lord. Following God should always trump your human ways and worldly desires because obedience is better than staying in sin. Pray that God will open doors for you two to start doing things in the proper order. Remember, blessing follows from obedience!

Kenady ended up being blessed by a living situation God orchestrated through a friend at church, who knew someone looking for a roommate for a short time. For a small fee, Kenady was able to move in with a lady from our church and thereby save some money for our wedding and future. Because we had a desire to do things God's way and were willing to do whatever it took, He honored us in an exceedingly abundant way.

Your story may not unfold like ours, exactly, but that doesn't mean God does not love you or that you are not blessed. You may have to sacrifice financially for a season. But I assure you, you will reap the blessings eventually. It's better to sacrifice money than to sacrifice your legacy by continuing generational cycles of dysfunctional families that do things out of order.

Also keep your boundaries in finances and legal accounts until you become one. It is not wise to tie yourselves up financially prior to marriage, even during an engagement season. Too often, we see couples prematurely getting on each other's phone bills, combining bank accounts, and adding themselves to each other's mortgages or leases, which can cause unnecessary strain. If those couples don't end up married, they will find themselves in sticky situations. Or worse, couples could feel trapped or pressured into marriage because of their financial ties. Thus, the wise thing to do is wait to join bank accounts and mortgages until after "I do."

Prior to marriage, we decided to create a document to show our respective finances—and that's it. We didn't start offering bank account numbers or investment accounts. This way, we showed each other that we were serious about transparency without crossing the line of merging our lives before it was time. It also allowed us to cast a vision for our financial future based on what types of places we could afford and how fast we could eliminate debt.

Let It Melt

"Shouldn't you test drive a car before you pull it off the lot?" A coworker posed this question to me when we talked about my stance as a virgin, and I've heard variations of the argument way too many times when discussing sex before marriage. This is the world's way of thinking about premarital sex. However, if you know the owner of the dealership and He knows your needs and what's best for you, it makes perfect sense to trust His judgment without going for any test drives. Learning each other on your wedding night or soon after is the beauty of consummation.

So the question remains: what if it's awkward that night? After marriage, couples go through a period of unlearning boundaries. I (Damien) was having strong feelings of affection for Kenady prior to marriage because naturally, God was growing us together. I managed these feelings by sharing them with Justin and praying that God would help me control my emotions. To Kenady, it might have felt like I was not interested, but in actuality, I was trying to turn off the part of me that yearned for physical intimacy. We called this the "ice age stage" because we sought to maintain our boundaries, keep any premature desires frozen and direct these desires toward God.

However, after marriage, couples have to learn that it's okay to cross the boundaries set in the courtship stage. You have to ask God to reprogram your mind and body toward your spouse. We call this the "global warming stage" because certain boundaries must melt. Sometimes couples struggle with intimacy at this point because they don't ask God for help. The world has perverted sexuality so much that many Christians don't realize it's healthy to ask Him for help. In fact, He wants to bless you as a presence in the sexual relationship between you and your spouse. Yet He's a pure "Gentlemen", He waits for you to invite Him.

The bottom line is, sex within marriage is worship unto God. It's the closest thing you can experience to the unity of the Holy Trinity. Sex outside of marriage, by contrast, is essentially like worshiping the devil, because sex is as much a spiritual act as it is an emotional and physical act. When you engage in it outside of God's intended design—that is, within a marriage between one man and one woman—you open up the door to demonic activity. This is why the Bible associates idol worshipping with orgies and sexual perversion (e.g., Galatians 5:19–21). It is so important to save sex until marriage in order to honor yourself, your future spouse, and most importantly, God. If you've already had sex prior to being married, it's not too late to turn your life around and save yourself until marriage. Be sure to repent of past sexual sins so that God can sever any demonic or soul-ties.

Sexual Dysfunction

In our churches, we don't talk enough about the fact that God Himself created sex and it was good. One of the biggest takeaways from the counseling we received on this topic is to not leave God or your faith outside the bedroom door. Sometimes, because of our perceptions based on the culture around us, media, or bad personal experiences, we might feel that sex is bad and we are naughty (as in, bad people) for having sex. We need to pray for the renewing of our minds in this area.

Although sex is a physical activity, its ramifications are emotional and spiritual as well. Again, sex inside of a biblical marriage is the closest thing we have to experiencing the Trinity, because God is involved as well. This is why it is also important to try not to violate your partner's wishes when having sex and to really communicate what you like and dislike in the bedroom.

Sexual problems and dysfunction are a bigger deal than most people admit. We don't want to be naïve in a world that is changing rapidly and, of course, is full of humans, who are sinful in nature. Sin is a cause of sexual dysfunction, but we want to offer solutions.

First, we believe as Christians that nonmarital sex, known as premarital sex, is wrong. Some people even have sex with animals, which is called bestiality, and with objects, which is called paraphilia. These acts are ungodly and disrespect the natural order of what God intended.

What about homosexual acts? Let me (Damien) tell you a true story. One day, I needed to run into a grocery store for a quick second. As I was exiting my car and heading inside, an SUV pulled out, right in front of the crosswalk. Out popped a grandson, his father, and his grandfather, while his mother stayed in the driver's seat to look for a parking spot. The grandson and grandfather headed into the store when all of a sudden, the grandfather said sharply to his grandson, "Son, we do not enter into exits." The grandson did an about-face, turned, and went through the designated entrance to the grocery store.

There is a legal order of all things. There are rights and wrongs. God created our bodies, and it's clear what each body part is used for. We don't have to do things or explore things that are not what the Creator designed us for. In short, we should never enter into exits. (Leviticus 18:22)

That said, not all of the dysfunction in our sexual experiences is attributable to sinful choices. According to the Global Study of Sexual Attitudes and Behaviors (GSSAB), 33 percent of women have sexual problems, compared to 18 percent for men. These dysfunctions can arise from natural, physical, psychological, drug/alcohol, or even relational causes. Problems can include erectile dysfunction, sexual disinterest, delayed orgasm, not finding sex pleasurable, depression, performance anxiety, or pain in having sex (mainly due to a problem with the female reproductive system not working), to name a few.[11]

To solve a problem, first, it's crucial to admit that there is a problem. Change happens over time, but it never happens if the problem is never addressed. Forty-three percent of men and women talk about their dysfunction with their partner.[12] I (Damien) remember I had a rideshare customer who got divorced because of sexual problems in his marriage. He vowed he was faithful to his ex-wife, but he had also vowed that he would never enter into marriage again without having had a sexual encounter with a woman first. (By the way, he was a professing Christian.) This is not a wise approach. He asked me my opinion, and I told him, "I don't know what you did, but I've learned that most people don't ask God into the bedroom before engaging in sexual intimacy with their spouse." He was quiet.

Secondly, I told him that although, for some reason, there is a stigma attached to receiving counseling for sexual problems, there is as strong possibility that the problem is not the male but a psychological problem from a past relationship incident that needs to be fleshed out (and flushed out) with a professional. And it is important to get in front of a Christian counseling professional who also understands the spiritual side of the matter. For more serious cases, physicians may need to get involved. Sex is deeply important in a marital relationship, and as disciples of Christ, we don't just shut down. We respect our partner and talk about important things honestly and openly, to serve one another.

Finally, as far as sex goes, how can a couple (male and female) enhance their sexual appetite? Dr. Bernie Zilbergeld says that to enjoy your sexual experience fully, you must explore "conditions for good sex," making sure you are "more relaxed, more comfortable, more confident, more excited, more open to your experience." [13]

Here are several things that should enhance sexual drive (for married couples), according to studies. Below, we paraphrase six research-based points about enhancing sexual drive, from *The Marriage and Family Experience:* [14]

Focus on proximity. We should seek to close the gap emotionally. Distance can breed disdain. Try to connect emotionally. This is especially important for women.

Focus on capability. This deals with our desire to have sex. It is important to talk (communicate) about each of your desires with your mate.

Focus on trustability. How do you build trust with your partner? You have to create a safe zone for emotional connectedness, in which your spouse feels worthy and has confidence that you won't judge, make fun of, or physically hurt him or her.

Focus on arousability. Arousal comes from the excitement and pleasure of sex. You have to view excitement as a gift, not a burden. Remember, your partner doesn't have to be sexual if he or she doesn't want to be. Continue to date your spouse. This is how you "keep the fire burning," as my (Damien's) late father would say.

Focus on physicality and mentality. It's very difficult to have pleasurable sex without having full buy-in. You don't want to show up "tired, ill, stressed out, pre-occupied, or under the influence of alcohol or drugs."[15]

Focus on positivity. It is essential to find positive environments and situations to have great sex. Foster an environment where your partner is able to feel secure expressing himself or herself openly to you.

Get Tested

Another subject that people don't often talk about is the importance of getting your blood tested, especially if you were sexually active before you committed to purity. This test should cover genetic as well as general health considerations. Kenady and I had a brief conversation early in our relationship about blood types, genetics, family history, and health status, but we weren't knowledgeable about all of the possible concerns. When our accountability brought up this topic again, later on, we saw this as confirmation that it was an important subject to explore and discuss.

We all have a past, and sometimes our mistakes have practical consequences even if we've repented of our sins and accepted Christ as our Lord. As a follower of Christ, you can still make a mistake—or suffer an experience outside of your control that affects your sexual health. For all of these reasons, it is wise not to enter into a marriage without knowing your status. We heard of one couple who were not sexually active during their courtship. However, after they got married, the wife started to feel sick and didn't know what was wrong. She ended up going to the doctor and found out that she had an STD. The only person she could have gotten it from was her husband, who believed he had contracted it from his last partner. Though it had been several years since he had slept with that person, the disease had remained dormant in him until he had sex again and passed it on to his wife. Though this wasn't intentional, it could have been prevented by getting tested and having the relevant conversations prior to marriage.

No matter what has happened in the past, be transparent with your potential partner on things that could potentially affect the future and family you build together, including STDs or genetic conditions. Such challenges aren't necessarily deal breakers for everyone. Both people in the relationship have freedom of choice and must determine for themselves, subject to God's counsel, what they are willing to enter a marriage with.

Personally, I (Damien) love the fact that I can join with another person and pray against the problems from our past. I love praying against generational curses in the bloodline. We must have a Kingdom mindset and not shy away from warring against our enemy. God is waiting on us to partner with Him to propel the Kingdom forward.

Remember, once you accept Christ, you are now in a covenant relationship with God the Father.

Courtship/Engagement Nuggets

Before we end this chapter, we want to offer you some one-liners you can take to the bank. These were some of the foundational lessons we learned as we got the opportunity to know one another better.

- Don't let social media and your phone keep you from socializing. When Kenady met my (Damien's) family, she put away her phone and engaged with my family.

- If you aren't drawing the other person closer to God, then you need to get out of his or her way.

- When it comes to finances and career, it's better to be in God's will than in God's way.

- Do you have knowledge, skills, and resources from which your partner can glean? Are you furthering your own development?

- Instead of comparing your relationship to others', measure your progress toward your goals in the different aspects of your relationship.

- Your relationship should not be a competition. We are in the body of Christ. We should rejoice when things are done to further the Kingdom because ultimately, it is God who gets the glory, not us.

- Don't withhold your thoughts and feelings about what you are going through. Your partner is not a mind reader. Communicate so that resentment won't build up.

- Avoid communicating sensitive information when you are exhausted or upset. Change the scenery. Go to a spot where you can have an intimate conversation. If you need to plan and inform the other person in advance, do so.

- Continue to be faithful in the "small"—because God is faithful through it all!

These nuggets, as you can see, are relevant (to varying degrees) within marriage as well as in courtship, engagement or just in life. Whether you're already married or not, we hope you apply wisdom to strengthen your relationship in God-honoring ways.

#COMPLETELYMARRIED

Chapter 8:

Premarital Counseling– Setting Up Your Marriage for Success

Every relationship is different. Each of us comes from a different background and has a different upbringing that affects our relationship and provides a unique perspective as to what a relationship should look like. For us, counseling represented an added layer of preventive care, like getting our teeth cleaned. Counseling is meant to help get to the root of self-sabotaging patterns, habits, and mindsets that you might be holding onto, before entering into a marital union. During this premarital period, it is important to refrain from becoming intimate sexually or creating soul-ties that cause emotional bondages, which would only add to the baggage each of us already carries.

Our church uses an excellent program called *SYMBIS* (Save Your Marriage Before It Starts, created by Dr. Leslie "Les" Parrott). Our counseling session was with Pastors Darius and Melba, who had been married for more than twenty-two years at the time of the counseling sessions. The pastor who was officiating the wedding wanted to have a couple of sessions with us, too.

One of the first questions the pastors asked us was, "When was your last disagreement or argument? And what was it about?" We don't really argue—which is neither good nor bad. It's how you communicate through frustrations that matter. One thing that we learned was to make sure we allow each other to share our whole heart when it comes to making decisions. Another lesson was that in making decisions, it's a blessing not to get your way all of the time.

As a couple, we agreed that once married, if there ever were a situation that required an immediate decision on which we couldn't agree, I (Damien)—as the man, who is the spiritual head of the household—would make the call. Kenady would submit to my decision, and we move forward with it. That said, it is proper for the husband to make a decision based on what is best for the couple or family as a whole, not on his own personal wants.

Now, if I were to make a decision that didn't turn out well, it would be an indication that I need to learn to lean more into what Kenady has to say. It would *not* be a time for Kenady to say, "I told you so!" and rebel the next time we have a serious decision to make. When mistakes are made, we will communicate more and grow closer from the experience. On the other hand, if it turns out I've made a good decision; Kenady will have had an opportunity to build her trust in my decision-making.

We both acknowledge that Kenady tends to be led by her feelings while I tend to lean toward facts. That's why our counselors gave us advice to help us navigate how God wired us. As we all know, feelings can change, which is where facts come into play. Kenady learned that she needs to slow down more, to review her schedule and think, before she makes decisions in the moment. Facts also need feelings: I was instructed to slow down and genuinely ask Kenady about decisions because her feelings are valid. Ultimately, facts + feelings = compassion, and this is the space Jesus landed in every time.

Another topic we talked about was money, which is one of the top reasons for divorce. The key to managing money within marriage is communication, so we sat down after our second counseling session and shared some things that we didn't know about each other's money habits. I (Damien) told Kenady that I tend to give money away to people on the streets who are in need, without telling other people about it. In my home growing up, my dad would say he wanted to budget, but behind the scenes he was helping everybody—using money that had been budgeted for other purposes, which frustrated my mom. I wanted to prevent that frustration in our relationship, so I started communicating with Kenady on big money moves, such as paying off debt. This new habit started to build trust between us on money matters, and Kenady reciprocated.

Another essential conversation in our premarital counseling was about expectations. We wanted to get downright honest about what was expected out of each of us. Our marriage would be for life, so we approached these conversations seriously and not just as excuses to talk and take up our (and our counselors') time. When examining expectations, we decided to filter them through three lenses: 1) Is the expectation communicated? 2) Is it realistic? 3) Does it even matter?

First, it's important to communicate an expectation before an argument develops. It's all too common to think an expectation of your future spouse is mutually understood, or that you've already addressed it, when in fact, you've never effectively communicated it to the other person. Likewise, because people change and grow, you have to communicate clearly when an expectation changes. If this communication doesn't occur, bitterness and unforgiveness can take root in your hearts, which will drive a wedge between you.

Secondly, are your expectations realistic? C'mon fellas, wanting your wife to cook a home-cooked meal three times a day when she has a full time job is unrealistic. So is expecting your husband to clean the whole house from top to bottom every day. These examples might seem like hyperbole (they should), but you get the point. Our expectations must be realistic so we can live in peace with each other. And with changes in season, such as during pregnancy, remember to reevaluate (and recommunicate) realistic expectations. Certain seasons may call one spouse or both to sacrifice in the realm of expectations.

Thirdly, does it even matter? Sometimes expectations can simply be petty. Maybe you like your pillows a certain way, or maybe your current, color-coordinated organizational system for your shoes won't work once you have to share closet space. These are far from life-or-death matters. We need to let such preferences go as the situation requires—and sometimes, it might be best not to bring them up in the first place.

If you are already married, you can also start to have these conversations (or have them again, if it's been a while). Wherever you are in your relationship, we pray you start communicating clearly, but compassionately, about your expectations.

During our last premarital counseling session with Pastor Marty (the officiate of our wedding), both of us had to reveal that our thought lives had not been so pure. Speaking for myself, I (Damien) was struggling, especially in the last thirty days before the wedding. We call this period "the thirst trap," during which the intensity of attraction grows. As our hugs got longer, we decided to meet only in public and tried to be intentional about steering away from certain topics. Even so, we frequently struggled and had to repent for some of the conversations we had. Kenady was definitely stronger than I was, though, and had to rebuke me on occasion. The enemy truly declared an all-out war against us so we would fall, but we participated and bear responsibility, too. Lust is no joke, even for people who have boundaries in place.

This is why accountability is so important to us. Again, we encourage you to be intentional to get counseling, before marriage as well as after your wedding day. We are extremely thankful to those who fought with us, prayed for us, and have walked the journey to the altar (and beyond) with us.

#COMPLETELYMARRIED

Part 3:
A Biblical Understanding of Marriage

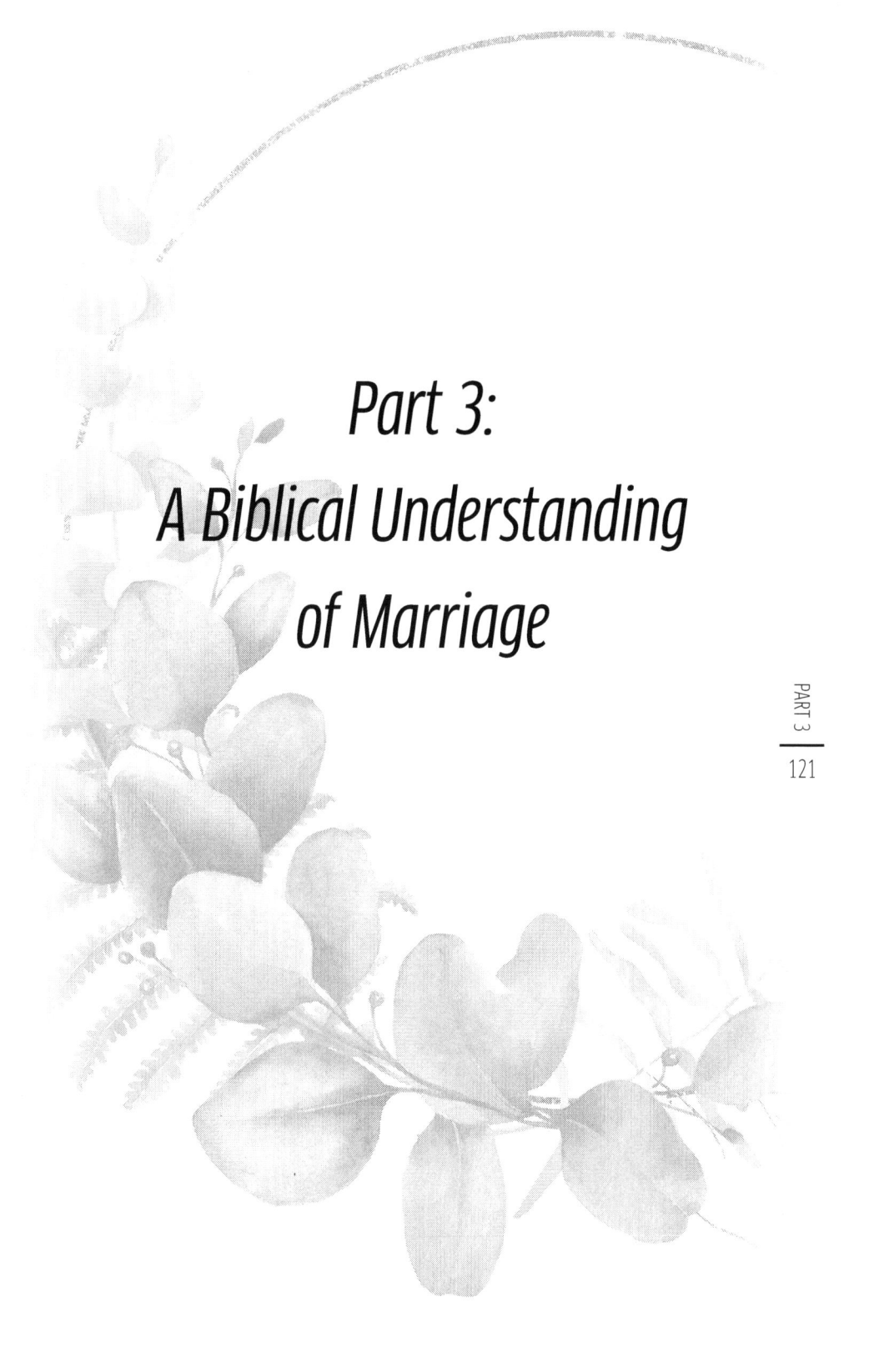

#COMPLETELYMARRIED

Chapter 9:
Back to the Original State

Creating a book like this can be challenging. Many potential distractions can get in the way of focusing on the task at hand. As we sat in the Sweet Hut restaurant in Duluth writing this book, there were times when we decided we needed a break.

During one break, Kenady pulled out her phone and asked me if I wanted to see her niece, Naomi. "No," I replied sarcastically. She then tried to offer me advice: if she ever asks me whether I want to see her niece, I should just respond, "Of course, babe!" In my head, I told her that I still didn't want to see the picture right then because I wanted to get back to work. Outwardly, I just smiled.

As Kenady jammed the phone in my face and forced me to see her niece, I noticed that Naomi had grown bunny ears. Kenady had taken a picture with a filter on her niece's face. In this social media age, we have grown accustomed to filters. Whether it's on Snapchat, Facebook, Instagram, or any other app designed for this kind of feature, our culture has fallen in love with not showing the simple, original image.

I told Kenady just to show me her niece in her original form. Kenady found pictures that had not been tampered with. And guess what? Her niece is gorgeous without any filter at all.

The lesson of the story is that we have to be okay with God's original. We don't think that all filters are bad, and they can add a little humor or spice to life, but whether it's bunny ears on your phone or makeup on your face, filters should not become your norm. We believe that God made you just as you should be. You are the original and unique, unlike anyone else in the world.

In this chapter, we felt it was important to go back to the Garden, where it all started for humankind, and talk about the original state of both male and female. This will give you perspective on why you might be drawn to act in certain ways, as well as what you need to do to get back in line with how God created us.

Our Original State

> Then God said, "Let us make man in our image, after our likeness. And let them have dominion over the fish of the sea and over the birds of the heavens and over the livestock and over all the earth and over every creeping thing that creeps on the earth." So God created man in his own image, in the image of God he created him; male and female he created them. And God blessed them. And God said to them, "Be fruitful and multiply and fill the earth and subdue it, and have dominion over the fish of the sea and over the birds of the heavens and over every living thing that moves on the earth."
>
> —Genesis 1:26–28 (ESV)

I know the tendency is to breeze through scriptures that we are familiar with, because I (Damien) do it, but it's important to slow down and see what God was communicating through Moses when he recorded these words. Several things stand out in this verse:

1. "Man," in this original sense, is made up of both male and female. Together, male and female make up mankind, or "godly offspring" (Malachi 2:15).
2. Male and female are made in the image of God, who is spirit. Our flesh is not made in the image of God, meaning we do not physically look like God.
3. Man (both male and female) was created to have dominion.
4. Male and female were created in community.
5. Male and female were created to be in a relationship and not alone.
6. Male and female were (are) blessed.
7. Male and female were given a command and purpose: "Be fruitful and multiply."

When God created mankind, he had both male (man) and female (woman) in mind. We see here that in the beginning, He didn't create any trans-human. We are wired either to be a male or a female. Though our spirits are not gender-based—there is no gender in heaven—here on earth, God gave us flesh and organs that identify us as either male or female. If you prick a baby's finger, you'll find that it has either two X chromosomes (female) or an X and a Y (male).[16] There has been talk in recent years about allowing kids to *choose* which sex they want to be, and to do so as young as the age of 4 or 5. However, if we teach them the Bible first, they'll have a better foundation to fight the enemy's attempts at identity fraud and identity assassination.

We have to understand that God called us to be the gender we are and He didn't make a mistake. There was a specific purpose He needed accomplished on the earth through mankind, so He said He would make a male (man) and a female (woman). Purpose always comes first; then God will create a successful environment for the purpose to thrive. God's holy presence is the place where you should camp out if you want to thrive in your purpose, just as a fish was created to thrive in water.

There is so much of deep significance in the list of points above, we could write a whole other book on it, but for our purposes here, we want to point three things in particular:

First, *our spirits were made in the image of God.* God is spirit, John 4:24 tells us. When you look in the mirror, is what you currently see the real thing or a reflection? It's an image, or reflection, of the real thing, as we're a reflection of God but are not ourselves God. He clearly says there is no god before Him (Deuteronomy 32:39). None of us is God, but we are spirit and possess a soul that lives in a body. Our spirit-man is the true essence of who we are and holds the key to our purpose on the earth. We are called to reflect and represent the very essence of God's Spirit, and one way—not the only way—we achieve this is through the gift of a marriage union between husband and wife. Not man and man, or woman and woman. There is a deep revelation that God intended to happen when two become one flesh through the marriage bed, with a man and women coming together.

Secondly, *we were made to be in community.* When God made us, He said, "Let *us* make man in our image" (Genesis 1:26 ESV, emphasis added). God the Father was conversing with the Godhead, including the Son and the Holy Spirit, to draw on elements of all of them to make us. In other words, He created us while in community with Himself, and significance happens in community. In community, great relationships can be formed to do wonderful things on earth—on purpose, for purpose, in purpose.

Third, *He blessed them.* God looked on to His creation with delight and adoration. When we come into Christ, we have to speak this truth: that we are too blessed to be oppressed by things that are outside of God's perfect will for our lives. He has blessed you to be more than conquerors, to have dominion and subdue the earth. No devil in hell can separate you from His love for you. Let me say that again: He loves you, and you are called to be blessed!

God made the physical man in Genesis 2:7: "Then the LORD God formed the man of dust from the ground and breathed into his nostrils the breath of life, and the man became a living creature" (ESV). This first man was without sin. He was naked and unashamed.

In Genesis 2:15–16, we learn some interesting things. We first learn that the man was in the presence of God Himself, learning his identity. God established three types of things with the man, in His presence, which are essential for the flesh to operate correctly: rules, responsibilities, and roles. These were created to protect the man's relationship with God. As part of this, the man was given work, which is important for self-discipline and self-control for both men and women.

A man's physical anatomy establishes that he was created to be a giver. If a man is selfish, he is not currently walking in his divine nature. Additionally, he was created to be tender, caring, and loving. In the Garden, God protected him, but he also learned how to protect the work and the land God had given him. However, he was also supposed to protect the word God had given him, which was not to eat the fruit off of the tree of knowledge. It is imperative to protect God's word! Lastly, the man learned faithfulness, headship (to be first), and leadership. In short, the man was expected to learn character traits similar to those of Jesus Christ.

The woman was created from the rib of the man in Genesis 2:21–23. God made the woman out of a need: Adam was alone, so God said, "It is not good for the man to be alone. I will make a helper who is just right for him" (Genesis 2:18 NLT). In Hebrew, that expression, "not good," meant that it was not profitable, useful, or fruitful. Adam could not be profitable, useful, or fruitful and take dominion alone or all by himself. Adam (man) was not an asexual being and could not reproduce to fill the earth without Eve (woman). Man and woman, together, are able to reproduce. Man and man, or woman and woman, cannot reproduce. Woman was not only made for reproduction purposes. Woman was also made as a helper, or what we sometimes call a helpmate. When studying the concept of a helpmate, you'll find that it actually indicates a superior being—not in value, but in status—who intentionally lowers herself and humbles herself to help another.

"Helper" also implies that she was to live harmoniously with the man. If there is always contention with your woman before you say, "I do," we would pray to see if this is truly the helper whom God called you to be with. Your helper is not perfect, but she is called to help produce so together you can accomplish God's purposes for you on the earth. She will be "just right," meaning suitable or appropriate, for you. Sometimes you might like a person, but it's important to pray to determine whether you are suitable for each other, to help each other with the purposes God intends.

The woman's physical anatomy says she is a receiver. She was created to nurture and to incubate a seed from the man. The woman was created to carry things; that's why God gave her a womb. In addition, after she carries these things, they should be presented back to the world better than she received them. The late Myles Munroe has observed that the woman can receive a seed from a man and produce a child.[17] She receives a godly vision and makes it into reality—like food into a meal or a house into a home. When you look at the woman's characteristics and how she is called to lower herself to help the man, you can see traits of the Holy Spirit.

Bad Fruit

Genesis 3:6 shapes each of our lives and the world we live in: "When the woman saw that the fruit of the tree was good for food and pleasing to the eye, and also desirable for gaining wisdom, she took some and ate it. She also gave some to her husband, who was with her, and he ate it" (NIV).

God gave me (Damien) a revelation about this whole scene. He asked me, "What was Adam supposed to do when Eve presented him with the fruit?" I thought about it, and then it came to me. I saw Adam slapping the fruit out of her hand because he remembered the command that God had given him.

Sometimes in our relationships, both man and woman can present their partner with "bad fruit" within a conversation. Maybe the bad fruit manifests as an insecurity, rejection, or negative self-talk. As soon as we recognize "bad fruit," Kenady and I immediately say, "Give me that fruit!" Then Kenady or I, whoever is the culprit at the time, holds out one or both hands as if to receive communion, so that the other person can swipe away the imaginary fruit. Yes, we laugh afterward, but it does help us stay positive and keep ourselves accountable regarding the things we say that can become harmful to ourselves or each other.

Bad fruit often has to do with perspective. You might have the best relationship in the world, yet your adversary whispers in your ear and says, "Look, you two should be doing that," or "Why isn't she/he saying ___ to you?" The enemy wants you to start comparing your relationship to others so that there can be division. But if you recognize the bad fruit early on, you can slap it out of each other's hands. I remember when Kenady told me that her dad did something every day and I should do the same. I quickly reminded her that I was not her father. Bad fruit! Ladies, never compare a man to a father. We should never seek to measure up to another man, but only to Christ. He is the one we should imitate. He created us with different personalities for a reason, to draw people to God and not to ourselves. For my part, I once started to joke about Kenady's past with alcohol. Bad fruit! It is never beneficial to make fun of the past while someone is sharing his or her heart. These are just some of the things we had to learn in our own relationship.

Swiping bad fruit from your partner is a lighthearted way to stay accountable with what you say or do. However, I think sometimes people succumb to the impulses of the flesh and instead of hitting the imaginary bad fruit, they hit each other. It is not okay to become violent in a relationship! We are speaking to both men and women here. Do not provoke each other, either. Be intentional and find the root of those feelings, whether rejection, abandonment, anger, rage, fear, control, or manipulation, just to name a few. Go seek counselors, or call the authorities if you feel that your life is in danger. Again, you should never lay your hands on a person if you truly love that person. Romans 12:18 says it plainly: "If it is possible, as far as it depends on you, live at peace with everyone" (NIV).

The Fall

The fall of man has caused a lot of heartache and bad fruit over thousands of years. When this event occurred, it created a ripple effect in humanity. Adam and Eve were proof that you can be living in the presence of God, without a sinful nature, and still make a bad decision. That decision ultimately led Adam and Eve to become spiritually separated from God, driven out of the Garden of Eden—essentially, ripped from the presence of God. However, before they left, God spoke these words in Genesis 3:16–17:

> To the woman he said, "I will surely multiply your *pain* in childbearing; in *pain* you shall bring forth children. Your desire shall be for your husband, and he shall rule over you." And to Adam he said, "Because you have listened to the voice of your wife and have eaten of the tree of which I commanded you, 'You shall not eat of it', cursed is the ground because of you; in *pain* you shall eat of it all the days of your life." (ESV, emphasis added)

For humanity, one effect of sin entering the world has been the compromising of the original rules, responsibilities, and roles of men and women. God never changed these original three R's of human nature, even when Adam and Eve sinned, but what did change was the pain involved. Now, yes because of historical and cultural developments, the roles of women have shifted over the decades and centuries. However the very essence of a woman, to be that nurture, incubator, and enhancer, should never change. The confusion of men trying to function as women, and women as men, is from the pain of sin but not from God. He just allows the pain so we can learn to draw closer to Him.

How else does the pain of sin manifest in our relationships? It has caused the man to rule over the woman, and it has also caused the woman to try to usurp the authority God had originally given the man to lead and be the head of the household. I (Damien) don't try to rule or control Kenady, and if that spirit of the flesh tries to rise within me to do so, I enter back into the presence of God.

You see, without a redeemed spirit (being born again), men and women will most likely be persuaded by the enemy to default back to the male and female's original fleshly purpose, which is merely to be fruitful and multiply—just having sex, like beasts, and dying without fulfilling any greater purpose. That original command to multiply was not just about bearing children but also about expanding the authority of the heavenly kingdom throughout the earth. By contrast, when unredeemed individuals become bored with sex and answer only to themselves, with no accountability, they start experimenting with their sexuality. In some cases, this has led to abusing others sexually and physically. It is also one reason why so many people nowadays are confused about their original sexuality. All of this underscores the need for us to show the unredeemed the way God originally created them and, when the time is right, to share the truth with them. As believers and disciples, we must continue to draw closer to God to fully understand what true love is and how to respect and serve our fellow man instead of taking advantage of other people.

Adam went through pain, but he did not stop living in his purpose. God allowed Adam to continue in his purpose when he named his wife "Eve": Genesis 3:20 says, "Adam named his wife Eve, because she would become the mother of all the living" (NIV). This is so encouraging to us, that we can still have purpose amid loss. We still can pursue what God calls us to do. Don't allow the pain to distract you or take your attention from the plan, purpose, or vision God has given you. When pain threatens to rob you of your vision, try to refocus on how big God is. Otherwise, you can miss seeing the very thing God is doing to bring you into your destiny. Focus on vision and purpose is key to all of your relationships.

After all, the story of mankind doesn't stop with the pain of the curse. Jesus didn't die just so we can remain the same. No, all humanity will return back to its original state, and the keys to this have been given to us through Jesus, who broke the curse. After the law of Moses was given to the children of Israel to give them structure, Jesus came to establish that the only way we can have grace to follow God's commands is through Him. As Paul writes in Galatians 3:13, "But Christ has rescued us from the curse pronounced by the law. When he was hung on the cross, he took upon himself the curse for our wrongdoing. For it is written in the Scriptures, 'Cursed is everyone who is hung on a tree'" (NLT).

So how, exactly, do you get back to the original state God intended for man and woman? For men, you have to study the life of Jesus and His relationship with the Holy Spirit. And for women, you should study the Holy Spirit and His relationship with Jesus. One thing is for certain: the Holy Spirit will never usurp the authority and headship of Christ, and Jesus will never try to dominate the Holy Spirit.

#COMPLETELYMARRIED

Chapter 10:
The Beauty of Covenant

My (Damien's) trip to Rome was the catalyst for several things in my life. As you read in the introduction, one of these things was the start of me finding my rib (a.k.a. my wife, Kenady). Another was my heart for family. My leader, Ty Buckingham, had a word of knowledge one day as we were in a session. I broke down and wept uncontrollably because God had given him knowledge of things that were hidden in the depths of my heart regarding the restoration of family. I literally hate divorce. Kenady and I want to see families in the body of Christ, and those outside the body, to be restored—but the only way is through Christ.

DAMIEN K. H. NASH AND KENADY NASH

Obedience and Boundaries in Marriage

Genesis 2:24–25 shows us a couple of things that I learned from my parents, which most children do not get to hear, because I was blessed with a father who studied and taught the Bible regularly.

> Therefore shall a man leave his father and his mother, and shall cleave unto his wife: and they shall be one flesh. And they were both naked, the man and his wife, and were not ashamed. (KJV)

My mother taught me the process of marriage, which is found within the scripture above. Here is the order my mother taught me: you should *leave* (your father and mother), *cleave* (marry your spouse, of the opposite gender), and *weave* (have physical intimacy). It's that simple, and you should strive to do it in that order. To clarify, to leave your father and mother is not to abandon and quit all duties of being a loving child. If they are sick and need care or need help around the house, you should help out. And the parents should never quit being parents of their adult children who ask for advice, guidance, or assistance. I am saying that they no longer have a responsibility to provide for you because you have become a man or woman and left their house to establish your own house.

In our broken world, we see marriages being defiled in so many ways. We see people today weaving, then halfway leaving their parents' house, and then cleaving. They never repent for being out of order before marriage, yet they still want God's blessings. For men, the manly thing to do is to humble yourself and repent, not make excuses. Otherwise, you will open your marriage to demonic attack. As Kenady told me when we discussed this particular chapter, "Don't be wifey if he isn't willing to lay down his life-y."

Later in my adult life, my father showed me something I'd never seen before in the scripture above. He had me read it first, and then he asked, "What do you see?" I didn't get a clear revelation, so he asked a different question: "Who was Adam and Eve's father and mother?" I responded with the only logical answer I could think of: "Umm, God." He said, "Exactly," and continued, "So how would Adam and Eve know this?" I knew this inference must have come to Adam and Eve through the Spirit of God. When Moses wrote the first few books of the Bible, he was writing on behalf of Adam, but ultimately on behalf of God. Adam and Eve didn't have parents, so in the beginning, God had to establish the order of the family—what should happen with the family until the end of time—as a prophetic utterance.

For governments to try to destroy this mandate is appalling, but the Bible leaves us with no excuses. Though you might not have had an earthly father and mother in your life to be great examples of what a godly marriage looks like, this scripture is telling you that neither did Adam or Eve, so you don't have any excuse not to do relationships the right way. If you have any need or void where you lack wisdom or real-life experience, if you seek God, He has the ability to give you wisdom, a prophetic word, or a word of knowledge about it—no questions asked! The Bible is clear, "But seek ye first the kingdom of God, and his righteousness; and all these things shall be added unto you" (Matthew 6:33 KJV). The problem is that we seek wisdom from too many of the created instead of the Creator. We have direct access to the source of all wisdom through Jesus Christ—so no more excuses!

Exodus 19 is a perfect picture of what our process of preparing for marriage as men and women of God looks like. We will give you more on this in Chapters 12 and 13, but we've found that the Bible offers us stories that are clear illustrations to glean from, to protect us from hurt, pain, and lack of peace in our relationships.

In the story below, we see Moses, the leader God chose for the people of Israel, take his priest and elders to give them clear instructions. They had just been brought to Mount Sinai, three months after leaving Egypt.[18] Before you get into marriage, you must learn how to be married to God, as Israel was married to God and His covenant.

> So Moses returned from the mountain and called together the elders of the people and told them everything the LORD had commanded him. And all the people responded together, "We will do everything the LORD has commanded." So Moses brought the people's answer back to the LORD.
>
> Then the LORD said to Moses, "I will come to you in a thick cloud, Moses, so the people themselves can hear me when I speak with you. Then they will always trust you."
>
> Moses told the LORD what the people had said. Then the LORD told Moses, "Go down and prepare the people for my arrival. Consecrate them today and tomorrow, and have them wash their clothing. Be sure they are ready on the third day, for on that day the LORD will come down on Mount Sinai as all the people watch. Mark off a boundary all around the mountain. Warn the people, 'Be careful! Do not go up on the mountain or even touch its boundaries. Anyone who touches the mountain will certainly be put to death. No hand may touch the person or animal that crosses the boundary; instead, stone them or shoot them with arrows. They must be put to death.' However, when the ram's horn sounds a long blast, then the people may go up on the mountain."

> So Moses went down to the people. He consecrated them for worship, and they washed their clothes. He told them, "Get ready for the third day, and until then abstain from having sexual intercourse."
>
> —Exodus 19:7–15 (NLT)

As we look at this scripture, we are extremely excited to find God highlighting His standard for the order of marriage, which can be achieved with the help and power of the Holy Spirit. The first major thing we see happening before the covenant is that the God of the universe desires to meet *intentionally* with us, and better yet, to introduce Himself to us. He could stay far away from us, but no, He wants to be close to us and meet with us regularly, face to face. Over time, this develops into a healthy friendship wherein you communicate with God and He with you—in which you both get to know one another more intimately in a spiritual sense.

Secondly, we see God looking for our "yes" to His covenant relationship before the law is given. God can introduce Himself, but we still could choose to reject Him. Whenever we see the word *covenant*, it indicates the existence of parties (which are the people and God), conditions, and blessing. In verse 8, we see the people enter into the covenant by saying, "We will do everything the Lord has commanded." One of the reasons our marriages or other relationships are falling apart is that we do not want to enter into an intentional covenant with God. We desire to do our own thing. My (Damien's) father would teach us something along these lines: "Most people are in a contact relationship. This relationship is based on convenience and not conviction. They are only looking to be in a physical relationship. Others are in contract relationships. These types of relationships keep their options open and are always looking for a way out. However, God is looking for a covenant relationship, which is the highest level of relationship." Have we committed to God first in all of our relationships and dealings?

The third major thing we see in this passage is the principle of God's covenant boundaries. God had specific boundaries set up for the people to follow before they encountered Him in the thick cloud. If they did not, they would have been stoned and shot by arrows. How can we apply this to our lives?

Before we enter into a marriage, we should establish clear boundaries—basically, what is off limits. You learned about ours earlier in this book. Remember, boundaries are put in place to protect your relationship before intimacy is established in marriage. God also wants to see if you will be obedient to His word. First Samuel 15:22 says, "To obey is better than sacrifice" (NIV). Psalm 16:5–6 (NIV) says, "LORD, you alone are my portion and my cup; you make my lot secure. The *boundary lines* have fallen for me in pleasant places; surely I have a delightful inheritance" (emphasis added). The Psalmist is looking at the boundaries as a blessing, not a hindrance. He knows that by staying within these lines, he will have everything he needs to live a secure life and receive an inheritance fit for a family member.

The boundary line was analogous to an engagement ring—a proposal, if you will. With it, the man says that the woman is off limits if (and only if) she says yes to his request. Then no one can touch her or pursue her any longer. She, in turn, is saying she is not looking to be pursued, when she wears her ring. If you don't wear your ring, ladies, don't get offended if men try to approach you. We understand that some ungodly men chase married or engaged women, but you have a better chance if you flash your ring finger and get to stepping.

The fourth principle we see is the test of time. God allotted three days for all of this to happen. Oftentimes there is a period before the

marriage, called the engagement. Courtship can be for an extended period of time, but usually it's best to check in with your accountability to see how the relationship is going. The engagement is when you send out the "save the date" invitations. God had already pursued the children of Israel and courted them. He then sent the "save the date" invitation through His prophet Moses.

The engagement period is a time where your patience is tested, whether in trying to get finances in order, get housing situated, or plan out the wedding. Typically, the engagement period is short: God's engagement period was three days, during which He desired His children to have an expectancy of worshiping Him intimately and also a joy to meet with Him by hearing His audible voice. Yes, God is omnipresent; however, this anticipated meeting would establish to the people that He was real and allow Moses to gain trust with the people.

I (Damien) want to take a quick *selah* (a holy pause) and speak to the men. Men, if you want to learn how to be a leader and have your lady trust in you as the head of the relationship, and eventually of the household, you must learn how to hear God's voice. The reason she may not trust you now is that you don't spend much time in the "thick cloud" that is the presence of God. It's evident when you have been listening to Him because your words will bear tangible fruit accordingly. The children of Israel followed Moses because he produced tangible signs.

Now, for the women: you get to help in this process by getting close enough to your man to make sure you are both hearing from God. The children of Israel were right there, not doing their own thing and trying to create their own vision behind Moses' back. Remember, two visions in any relationship create division, which can lead to divorce. And God hates divorce.

The fifth principle we see here is that of preparation. Moses was called to consecrate the children of God. To consecrate is to devote something to God as sacred.[19] Why was this necessary? Because they were about to hear the audible voice of God, which would lead to more trust from the people. God commanded Moses to tell the people to clean their clothes. They didn't have clean clothes lying around since they had just come out of Egypt, so they cleaned the clothes they had. God wanted His people to be purified both spiritually and physically before He met with them. On that note, when you are about to enter into a union, you should also check your hygiene. Clean yourself up, as Ruth did for Boaz. If you can afford to buy new clothes on your budget, great, but regardless, don't just say "He/She had better like me for who I am." It is appropriate to make yourself presentable for your future spouse.

Lastly, we see the principle of abstaining from sexual intercourse. God told the elders, "Do not touch your women." This was an odd command because sexual intercourse was a gift given by God, but God had a purpose for everything. Coffman's Commentaries states, "However, in the culture of those days, there was a special reason for this injunction. Throughout Canaan and among all the surrounding nations the usual religious service was an orgy in which sexual indulgence was a normal part." Before you get married, it is appropriate to practice self-control because you should always desire for your spirit to rule over fleshy things.

Soul Mates

I (Damien) personally have not liked the term *soul mates* since learning about and experiencing soul ties. The soul comprises the mind, will, emotions (feelings), imagination, heart, and desires. What

I have found out from trial and error is that a lot of times, our minds need some renewing. We must spend the appropriate time allowing God to take us through that process. Time and time again, when people seek a relationship with a like-minded individual (soul mate), I have seen the relationship end with a lot of unnecessary pain because their souls are not renewed and their spirit may not be regenerated. Most people, both in and out of church circles, aren't ready to do what it takes to have a healthy soul. When your soul is healthy, your life will start moving toward Kingdom relationships.

Your soul is like a computer hard-drive. I love something I once heard the late Myles Munroe say on this subject: "There is only two ways to restore your soul. First, you can install the original software, which is the Word of God." One of my favorite scriptures, that we all should try to memorize, is Joshua 1:8 (ESV), which reads, "This Book of the Law shall not depart from your mouth, but you shall *meditate* on it day and night, so that you may be careful to do according to all that is written in it. For then you will make your way prosperous, and then you will have good success" (emphasis added).

The word *meditate* in this scripture is related to a term for sheep that chew their food, swallow it, and regurgitate it right back up. Yes, this is graphic, but necessary for your understanding. The Word of God needs to brush over your mind, will, and emotions (your soul) continuously when wrong thought patterns and feelings start entering your life. That's one way to restore your soul-hardware.

Secondly, Munroe said you might need a whole new hard drive, meaning that you must be born again. If you are not saved, you will never come fully into the knowledge and peace of God, and it is foolish to enter into a relationship without God's help. You might see unsaved people look okay on TV, the internet, or social media, but they inevitably have a piece missing that cannot be ignored.

Mark 8:36 is very clear: there's no benefit to gaining the entire world while losing your soul. No matter what your life on earth is like, if your soul remains un-renewed, you will end up eternally separated from God, which is called hell. However, we are here to tell you there is good news—the gospel of Jesus Christ. He came to set you free, restore your relationship back to the Father, and restore your soul into the peace of salvation. Romans 10:9 says, "If you confess with your mouth that Jesus is Lord and believe in your heart that God raised him from the dead, you will be saved" (ESV).

We have all made mistakes and sinned. Sin means we have missed the mark. We have all lied, cheated, stolen, or otherwise failed to obey God's commands. In our sin, we are out of fellowship with the Holy God, and the only way back to Him is through His one and only Son, Jesus. If you have not made a decision for Christ, we encourage you to offer a prayer of repentance for your sins and acceptance of Christ as your Savior, and thereby restore your soul's relationship with God.

If, like me (Damien), you don't prefer the term *soul mates*, what should you use? When I wrote out a list of possible terms with my sister-in-law back in 2008, one of the things on my list was "My Rib." That's right—I was not just looking for someone who could match all of my criteria on the outside but someone who had a piece of me internally. God did not remove a soul from Adam after all; he removed a rib. And I can say without a shadow of doubt, Kenady Cheyenne was and is my rib. I moved from being a womb mate with Julien, my twin brother, to being a rib mate with my wife, Kenady.

God gave me a revelation on this subject several years before I even thought about writing this book. During my study and meditation time, He asked me about the time Adam was asleep (Genesis 2:21): "Why did I put the man to sleep?" Then, as I studied, I received some amazing insight: your life as a single person is the time when you should be asleep (or resting) in God while waiting for your mate. However, since you've decided to stay awake, fixated on your singleness, you feel the pain of God's surgery as His plan to bring you your spouse is in progress. So you are feeling the pain God never intended for you to feel, of a spouse being brought to you.

For one, you worry about being alone, which is painful. Moreover, God needs to "remove a rib" from the man and give it to his wife, which manifests as her desire for him (see Genesis 3:16). This can be a painful process for both people if you try to control it—to resist the operations God is performing. So, why is it so painful to find a wife nowadays? Because you, especially men, are not resting in God! The healing and recovery from surgery take longer when you're awake than when you are asleep.

When you read Genesis 2:21, notice that God did not take out a soul, but a rib, and then closed the place back up. Likewise, you want God to close the compromised places in your flesh before your rib comes parading into your life. Pray that all fleshly sin, especially sexual sin, will be removed from your life. If that area is not appropriately confronted and closed, it can significantly decrease your capacity to love your spouse intimately, the way God established for us in the beginning.

If you don't remember anything else from this chapter, remember that God desires to bless us; however, the condition is that we adhere to the requirements of His covenant. We cannot expect God to fulfill His covenantal blessing when we have violated His requirements. God established orderly arrangements for things for our sake, not His. He wants us to receive the fullness of our inheritance, but we have to be mature and lean on His word when times get tough and when our feelings, emotions, and flesh rise up, drowning out the Lord's voice in our lives. Yes, being in a relationship is a wonderful thing, but our covenant relationship with God should always supersede our earthly relationships. Keeping our relationship with Him first will always benefit our relationships here on this earth.

Chapter 11:
Leading and Submitting

I (Damien) don't think men are the only ones who have the ability to lead. We see evidence in the Bible that there were competent women leaders. However, I do believe the man is supposed to be the head of the home. There is a difference between being the head and leading. (I speak at length about headship in Chapter 12.)

As disciples of Christ, we have to recognize that we are called to lead in every area in our lives to bring God glory and joy. No matter what industry you have been called into, or if you are male or female, you are meant to shine your light in leading others to follow Christ. We've spoke already about the origin of the male and female and their roles. We are called to lead from these respective roles, not diminishing what God has created us to be. The Bible is clear: "So whether you eat or drink or whatever you do, do it all for the glory of God" (1 Corinthians 10:31 NIV). The word "you" here does not have a gender associated with it. We can each lead in whatever we do, to the glory of God.

What Does It Mean to Lead?

So, how do you lead?

My (Damien's) father, the late Rev. John Al Nash, taught on leadership all the time, and he was a master teacher, his students at Beulah Heights University shared with us. He defined a leader, especially a person who has accepted Christ as Lord and Savior, as a person who influences other people to accomplish godly purpose by the power of the Holy Spirit. They have vision, character, and integrity, and they are willing to take risks. He also gave his students the following acrostic to help them remember what it is that we are all called to be:

Laborers: The Bible says, "For we are labourers [co-workers] together with God: ye are God's husbandry [field], ye are God's building" (1 Corinthians 3:9 KJV). God has called us to work alongside Him in the field to which He has called us. In short, leaders are people who continually seek the work of the Lord. They understand that Christ must be the foundation of whatever they do. If you build anything on any other foundation, no matter what it is, it will ultimately fail. As a leader, you must know this and lead your followers accordingly, so they can achieve their life purpose, too.

Empowerers: If you want to become the leader God is calling you to be in your home, as a man or as a wife, you must learn how to empower. The Bible gives us a great example of this in Matthew 9:37–10:1, which reads: "Then he said to his disciples, 'The harvest is plentiful but the workers are few. Ask the Lord of the harvest, therefore, to send out workers into his harvest field.' Jesus called His twelve disciples to him and gave them authority to drive out impure spirits and to heal every disease and sickness" (NIV).

Jesus understood the law of multiplication. Yes, He was God, but He came as a man, and He knew His greatest weapon was found in us.

If we are unified, the anointing, authority, and power of God will flow through us to do His work. Jesus saw the few who were ready for the calling and gave them authority. He empowered them. We must find the few who are serious about the call and pour our lives into them. When we empower, we are giving the people we lead the confidence to take the torch and run with it.

Ambassadors: A term that is often underestimated in importance is ambassador. Second Corinthians 5:20 says, "So we are Christ's ambassadors; God is making his appeal through us. We speak for Christ when we plead, 'Come back to God!'" (NLT). The word ambassador is extremely weighty on my soul whenever I hear this scripture quoted. It has several meanings, but the bottom line is that we represent one Kingdom in another kingdom. Once you have been born again, you have authority to represent the kingdom of God here on earth. In my home, I must be an ambassador of God toward my wife—and vice versa. Kenady does not get a pass here. Regardless of how one of us is acting in the moment, the other person should represent God's kingdom well. This will also help the offending person realize that he or she might be out of line, repent, and turn back to God. This term does not just hold weight in your home but also at work, at the grocery store, at the mall, and at your place of worship.

Demonstrators: Lastly, leaders must demonstrate what is being taught. I have been coached by several other men over my life. The best coaches to me were the one who would dive in with us from time to time and demonstrate the instruction they were speaking at us. This gave me confidence: "If this old man can do what he's asking of me," I'd think, "I know I can." Leaders do not look at demonstration grudgingly but as part of serving the overall mission to help us succeed. They are not looking for the credit, either, but giving the spotlight to the mentee or disciple to receive the reward.

It would be difficult for me to follow a minister who did not practice (demonstrate) what he preaches, especially when it comes to healing the sick or casting out devils. Jesus did not just talk about these things; He demonstrated that they can happen. He was the ultimate servant-leader. Likewise, we as leaders must seek to practice what we preach. We must also believe in what we teach or else risk forming disciples who are weak and not themselves ready to lead. We must lead like Jesus if we are going to be effective, no matter what time, place, or situation we find ourselves in.

What Does It Mean to Submit?

What does submission look like? Ephesians 5:22–23 states, "Wives, submit yourselves unto your own husbands, as unto the Lord. For the husband is the head of the wife, even as Christ is the head of the church: and he is the saviour of the body" (KJV). We decided to put that verse in this chapter because submission happens under covering. I (Damien) am now placed as a covering over Kenady. We recognize that this word *submission* has been dragged through the dirt so much in the context of the twentieth- and twenty-first-century church, as even the church has used it incorrectly. In fact, we can already see the eyes rolling as we type this. But hold on!

Too often, lack of understanding and proper explanation has led godly women to buck at their husbands when any attempt at exercising or establishing authority has been offered in the home. And we can't forget about men who have tried to use this word *submission* to manipulate their women into improper sexual activity or other behavior. As a result, this word has left a bad taste in the mouths of many individuals, who have removed it from their relationships and homes accordingly. We personally would not be surprised if the concept of submission, along with communication difficulties, has been a leading factor in divorces over the last couple of decades. However, misunderstanding and confusion can stop today, right here.

I (Damien) remember how worn out I felt on one particular day toward the end of my mission trip in Rome. Our days were long. We were usually up by 7 a.m. and then got back in bed at 1 a.m. or 2 a.m. I decided not to attend the mandatory meetings, but to take a much-needed nap instead. Even though it might have been deserved—and again I was burnt out—I should not have just skipped these meetings. Pertinent information was given in these sessions for our nightly ministry outings on the streets, like where to go to meet your group, what area of town you were going to, and whether you might be accompanying any other group.

As I was sleeping, I heard an audible voice. (This is not usual to me. I usually get small impressions.) The voice says, "There's blessing in submission." I felt the love of the Father intensely in this moment, and conviction filled my soul. You see, God doesn't want to hurt us but to teach us how to be more like His Son. Even Jesus submitted to His cousin John the Baptist. If Jesus could submit, so can we. After I got up and repented to God, I went to my team lead, whom I was waaay older than, and I apologized. They had worried because I was one of the elders in the group, and I understood then that no matter my age, if authority is placed over me, I shall submit. Come to find out, our group, which had some of the youngest members out of over six hundred participants, saw the most salvations over the period of fifteen total days. We witnessed several healings as well. Praise Jesus! What I want you to remember from this story is simply that there's blessing in submission.

For the Christian, the disciple who has surrendered his or her life to Christ, one of the definitions of submission can be found in

Ephesians 4:2–3: "With all lowliness and meekness, with longsuffering, forbearing one another in love; endeavouring to keep the unity of the Spirit in the bond of peace" (KJV). To submit as a Christian woman is actually a position of love. You are taking a lower position (*sub-*) under the **mission** in your home. And the mission of every Christian home is that the man should be intentional to lead like Christ.

Additionally, submission means the woman is responding to what the man is putting out. The woman is not commanded to love but to respect the husband, which is a sign of love. The man, in turn, is commanded to love as Christ loves the Church, which in turn will elicit respect from the woman. No matter if you're from an Eastern or Western culture, this is the Bible, the Word of God, which is our constitution, and we now follow the Kingdom culture.

Men are the initiators and givers. Women are to receive and respond to what the husbands give out. The way we respond to Christ's call for our lives is the same way women choose to respond to their husbands in love. However, if a woman is cold toward her husband, or standoffish, it is likely a direct reflection of what the man is putting out. In the next chapter, we'll examine what biblical wisdom says about being the kind of husband God intends.

Chapter 12:
How to Prepare to Be a Husband

Before we get into the various biblical principles related to being a husband, I (Damien) think it's imperative to dissect that word and define it. Interestingly, our noun *husband* is related to the old-fashioned verb *husband*, which means to grow (as a farmer does) or steward (care for and be responsible for) something. In heterosexual monogamous relationships, one cannot hold the title of husband unless there is a ceremony that brings two parties together. The parties include *only* two human beings, one being born a male and the other being born a female, who have stayed that way through their entire lives.

Over time, different cultures (including the present culture) have tried to rearrange or redefine the institution of marriage. However, looking at the Bible, the way I describe it above is the way God set it up, and I don't see any reason why we should try to pervert (change) it.

You can use HUSBAND as an acrostic or mnemonic device to better understand the different aspects of what it means to be a husband according to the Bible.

Head

In mid-June of 2018, I was sitting in the living room, talking to my mentee. This young man and I were discussing another friend, who had just had a baby out of wedlock, when my mentee said, "If I had a baby, I would never fail her." I said, "*If?* No, you don't start there or say that."

He tried to rebut me by saying, "Damien, we are human. I might mess up—you never know. I might find a girl, get too close, and become intimate. And, you know, have a baby."

I said, "*What?* That's the dumbest thing I've heard. No. You will not mess up." Then I continued sternly, "You need to tell yourself, I will not have a baby until marriage. I will not mess up." And I walked away.

Seconds later, he said, "Damien, you are right. I don't know what I was thinking. I will not mess up, and I will have a baby after I am married. I rebuke what I said in the name of Jesus."

The enemy wants to cut off the head of the family, as God created the man to be. As David proclaimed to Goliath, "I will strike you down and cut off your head!" in 1 Samuel 17:46 (ESV), we can see the enemy adopt similar ferocity toward men in Western culture today. The attack on men as head of the family has reached an epidemic scale.

My mentee's initial mindset is rapidly taking over and growing within the souls and heads of many young men. As a culture, we are doing things out of order, growing apathetic about God's way, and we think it's all right. But this is not okay, and it takes real men to stand up against the wiles of the enemy. When we get our heads right, we can prepare to be the head of our households, as God has called us to be.

Ephesians 5:21–33 is a go-to passage in preparing, as men, for marriage. I don't think you should get married and then learn how to be a husband. This is why I am writing this chapter, for those of you who desire to be married one day. It can also be helpful for those who are married and need to reset their mentality.

Ephesians 5:23 says, "For the husband is head of the wife, as also Christ is head of the church; and He is the Savior of the body" (NKJV). Why the head? The head is mentioned more than four hundred times in Scripture. For that matter, several people were beheaded in Scripture (Goliath, John the Baptist, Saul) as an expression of complete (earthly, at least) victory over an opponent.

The head also features in rituals for anointing or mourning. Leaders might bless or anoint individuals by laying hands on their head or pouring oil on the top of their head. In the case of mourning or grief, people in biblical cultures would throw dirt or ashes on their heads.

Paul obviously had some of these meanings in mind as he wrote the scripture above. Christ is presented as the leader but also as a provider in this specific verse, which helps us dissect the meaning for ourselves. We see that Paul wants us to recognize that Christ is the standard for leadership and provision in the home. If Christ is the standard, you are not supposed to be just any leader, but a supernatural, spiritual leader.

So, what are some characteristics of a spiritual leader?

Spiritual Leaders

One of the first things a spiritual leader does is *pray*. If you want to be the real head of the household and look attractive to your wife, learn how to pray. As a former prayer team leader, I can tell you I felt incredibly sad when I walked into a room and only saw one or two guys praying alongside ten to fifteen women. Men, we have to make it our mission to learn how to seek God's face for His will and vision for our family. We must learn to yearn to communicate with our Father. I personally love praying and talking to God.

So where do you start? Pray that His Holy Spirit comes upon you. Pray for His protection over your family. Pray for His wisdom in decision-making. Pray that He reveals a plan for you to direct your family this year in establishing His kingdom here on earth. Start there!

Secondly, spiritual leaders *work hard*. Jesus was a carpenter before His ministry started. He was used to working hard with his father Joseph, and then his promotion came. Two words associated with the kind of work ethic Jesus practiced are *integrity* and *faithfulness*. Hard work produces these characteristics. We see numerous stories in the Bible in which God acknowledged those who were faithful in their work, whether it was Adam, Moses, David, or Martha. These and many other biblical men and women worked hard, and God rewarded them in His own special way, such as in the form of a position or a revelation. Ask yourself: *Do I work hard? Am I faithful or a flaker? Do I work with integrity and character, or do I like to cut corners?* I understand men may want some downtime on occasion, but commit to getting off the remote control, social media, or game controller and going to work on the things to which God has called you. I know this chapter is for my brothers in Christ, but my sisters can also benefit from this as you prepare to be the best spouse you can be.

Third, spiritual leaders learn how to *communicate*. Communication is not a one-way street. It takes two parties to communicate: you have a listener and a speaker. In coaching, we go further and call it active listening. The better you are at listening, or decoding the message, the better communicator you will become. Everyone can become better at this. Some tips that I have learned over the years—which are especially challenging for me, by the way—include:

- Turn your full attention to the person. Turn off the TV and do not scroll through your social media feed.

- Verbally respond by making appropriate sounds or utterances like "okay" or "really?" This is to let the speaker know you are attentive (and alive).

- Wait until the other person is finished before trying to correct something or give your opinion.

- Repeat what the person said back to him or her by saying, "What I heard you say is,_____. Is that correct?"

- Ask if the other person wants to know your opinion or just wanted you to listen.

Again, I am not good at this yet. I have caught myself several times scrolling through social media while Kenady was talking. Don't take for granted the people in your life or our conversations with them. You must continue to value them—and show that you do.

Spiritual leaders also *provide*. As the head of your household, you don't simply *have* to, but rather, you *get the honor* of providing for your family financially, as well as providing security and protection. With societal changes, this might look different in different households; after all, there are women in executive roles who make seven figures. To this point, I just encourage you to live wisely, save, budget, and communicate how to handle a loss of position. You do not want to be caught off guard if there is an economic downturn. Ultimately, the man must be prepared to assume the position of provider if he is physically and mentally capable of doing so.

Furthermore, spiritual leaders make *mistakes*. The reality is that we are in a fallen world and our sanctification is a process, meaning we have not arrived in our perfected form. In fact, the Bible tells us completion to perfection comes after death, with Christ's return, when we will get our heavenly bodies. However, this does not give you an excuse to live any way you want, either. It shows you a path to continue to become all that God has created you to be, as you strive for more significance than mere success. With that said, you should follow these quick three steps when, not if, you mess up:

- *Admit.* Take responsibility. Don't run from it or lie about it; face it. The Bible is clear: confess your faults to one another.

- *Accept consequences.* As the spiritual leader of the home, if there is a legitimate penalty or punishment for your actions or failed leadership, accept it. You should take it on the chin.

- *Rectify.* Try your best to learn everything that went wrong and work with a team of people (accountability), if need be, to try your best to fix the error.

I had to close the door on past relationships by intentionally calling different women with whom I'd had inappropriate interactions. I apologized and released both of us. Yes, it was hard, but it's necessary as the head and a leader that you bring the least possible amount of mess into a union. If I can do this, so can you. No matter if you are a man or a woman, release the soul ties that are keeping you bound. I admitted my portion and didn't cast the blame.

And guess what, some of these relationships ended—but not on bad terms. There was no bad blood; rather, it was like we did not need to talk anymore. Sometimes friends are connected by sin, which can also be seasonal. Release the sin, rectify the matter, reconcile, and move forward. Sometimes moving forward leaves others behind.

Upright

In Ephesians 5, Paul implores the men of Ephesus to lead their wives like Christ led the church. One thing that continued to stand out in my mind as I meditated on this passage was the name *Christ*. Paul didn't choose exceptional Bible characters like David, Moses, Isaiah, or Elijah as the example; he chose Christ. There was something significant about Christ that was unlike all the other people in the Bible. He successfully navigated being one hundred percent man and one hundred percent God for over thirty-three years! He was the Messiah, the Anointed One. These are all appropriate names for Him, but I want to shift our focus toward the type of character that Christ displayed. His character was flawless, literally. He was a man without sin who became sin for us. I would define *character* as the moral code you live by after the fame has vanished, the lights are off, and the excitement has passed. Before we go any further, take a quick *selah* and ask yourself the important question: how is your character?

Psalm 92:15 says, "The LORD is upright; he is my Rock, and there is no wickedness in him" (NIV). Honestly, can you say we are striving to live an upright life as you are preparing for marriage? The word *just* is another way of saying "upright" in this sense. *Upright* literally means to stand straight, of course, but figuratively, it refers to a moral person—someone with integrity. The Bible says that Jesus Christ lived with perfect integrity and always took the morally straight path. He lived a righteous life by choice, through the Holy Spirit.

It is imperative that you, as a disciple of Christ, study and understand the attributes of God. Omnisapience, which means that God is All-Wise, is one of His many characteristics. These attributes can offer divine insight in the tough moments of your life. Sometimes you might have sought people instead of God when going through difficult things, but people can be very unwise. They may try to analyze or explain your situation in a way that brings you temporary comfort, but over the years, I have seen, heard, and at times been guilty myself of saying things that sound smart yet were ultimately damaging to my brother or sister in Christ. And I repent of that. I admit now that I lacked the wisdom and a full understanding of the situation but was too prideful to say, "I don't know." Despite my shortcomings, God Himself has all wisdom and wants to help you live uprightly like His Son, Jesus Christ. Remember that in every situation, Jesus chose the best way to accomplish the best end—and that's what living uprightly means.

Several of God's attributes can contribute to living an upright life, but two that stand out for us are God's omniscience and His omnibenevolence.

You cannot be all-knowing, which is the definition of omniscience. However, you can access God-given knowledge by studying His word and communicating with Him through prayer. Studying the Bible is not just for information: it enables you to glimpse how God thinks, as well. As the future spiritual leader of your home, make sure you have your family's best interests at the forefront of your mind by seeking and spending time in the presence of the All-Wise, All-Knowing One. This is not just you trying to grow toward godly perfection but also you trying to seek the most effective ways of leading your home and living righteously for your family. Your decisions you make while away from your family are just as important as your decisions in front of them.

What do you do when an old flame reaches out to you on your phone or a social media platform? What are the proper steps when porn pops up on your devices? What should you do if you got overpaid on your paycheck? These are all questions that can be answered through the reading of Scripture and understanding the consequences of making the wrong decision. I have no doubt that really diving into the Scriptures will hone your wisdom antenna. You can start in Proverbs—the book of wisdom.

God's attribute of omnibenevolence is another key component of living an upright life. God is All-Good and All-Loving, and because of this, He not only knows the most effective (right) way, but He also knows the best way to reach the best end result. Therefore, love should spearhead your character. The starting point isn't how much you love your family, either. That is a piece of it, but it's how much you love God that's fundamental. John 14:15 (BSB) says, "If you love Me, you *will* keep My commandments" (emphasis added). To live an upright life requires loving God first.

I once heard a pastor say, "If we don't know how to love, we can't call ourselves Christian." I think that is true. Living upright must stand on the foundation of love—and God is love, 1 John tells us. Todd McIntyre, men's pastor at Gateway Church in Texas, once said, "The most loving, which turns into the best thing you can do for your future family, is to learn how to protect them from all of our evil desires."[20] And let's be honest: we have a lot of evil desires that rise up inside us from time to time. We have to seek the love of God to be the spiritual leaders God is calling us to be in the home, and we should seek it before "I do." That said, is it too late for married couples? No! I just don't want you to experience or cause unnecessary pain because you would not heed this advice beforehand. I myself am still learning, of course, as I seek God's love while He teaches me how to love Kenady, but I know that it means forgiving quickly and avoiding bitterness. Once you truly understand your identity in Christ, fleshly and spiritual evil are easier to avoid.

Servant Heart

In Ephesians 5:25, Paul instructs, "Husbands, love your wives, just as Christ also loved the church and gave Himself for her" (NKJV). I want to focus now on the word *gave* in this particular verse. When we look in the Strong's Concordance for some insight into the original language, we see "to surrender, to yield, and commit."[21] Jesus Christ committed His life to the body of believers, His church, and we as men get to do the same for our wives. In this, Jesus displayed the heart of a servant—and more than that, a suffering servant. Like a Lamb, Jesus was led to the slaughter for our sins and so He even served us in death! That was true love.

Now, having a servant heart doesn't begin automatically when you say your vows, say "I do," and kiss your beautiful bride. Again, I want to help you now to become the best man and husband for your future spouse. The Bible, especially the New Testament, shows the importance of being a servant, but our culture has marked a servant as not being of high position. The result is situations where people act rude and display a sense of entitlement. Yet we are all equal in value in the sight of God, and what's more, as a spiritual leader, you get to proclaim that servanthood is the best 'hood!

Whether you're pre-married or already married, if you haven't yet taken on this servant heart, don't fret! You can literally start changing today.

Know Who the Owner Is

Philippians 2:5–7 says, "In your relationships with one another, have the same mindset as Christ Jesus: who, being in very nature God, did not consider equality with God something to be used to his own advantage; rather, he made himself nothing by taking the very nature of a servant, being made in human likeness" (NIV).

The first principle we see Jesus live out so gracefully is to know His position as a Son. He was the only person in history who could have elevated Himself because He was God. He took the position of a servant, however, to show us that we can do the same.

Knowing the Love of the Owner/Father

"Beloved, let us love one another, for love is from God, and whoever loves has been born of God and knows God. Anyone who does not love does not know God, because God is love" (1 John 4:7–8 ESV). Scripture tells us that God loved the world so much, He gave us His Son for our sins (John 3:16). We as men should settle on this fact as the truth. God loves us no matter our adolescent experience with our natural father. Because of His love for us, we can now go out and serve those God has placed in our path. Doing so is only going to help you as you prepare for your wife.

I personally am intentional about keeping certain individuals around me, both to keep me grounded and to keep me humble. My friend Gordon Cone is a servant who serves wholeheartedly. He wants to be great in the Kingdom, and he challenges me to continue to have the mindset of a servant, too.

Recently, we were at an event here in Atlanta. It was late at night, and we had been there for more than four hours. However, the church was trying to set up chairs for their weekend service. Now, I was a visitor, and I'll be honest with you, I was ready to go. However,

Gordon was like, "Let's help them." I was reluctant at first, but then I saw a majority of the helpers were the women of the church. I thought a couple of men should help as well.

You see, Gordon knows the love of the heavenly Father, I am certain, which makes him have a heart for sharing that love in acts of service toward others. What about you? Do you know the love of the Father?

Know Thyself

> Jesus said to him, "I am the way, and the truth, and the life. No one comes to the Father except through me. If you had known me, you would have known my Father also. From now on you do know him and have seen him."
> —John 14:6–7 (ESV)

We can't effectively serve out of our insecurities. We have to know ourselves and be comfortable with who God created us to be. Do you recall kids making fun of you at school or the playground, whether it was about how you dressed, your hair, or even your personality? You may have noticed that it doesn't stop as you get older. Have you experienced people picking on you lately? Even when you are grown, the enemy will bring random people into your life to speak ill of you. But remember, God values you, and He is in love with you and your personality! You, too, need to fall in love with what God made—so much that you are willing to give it away.

What are you good at doing? What gifts, abilities, and skills has God given you to serve humanity? For me, one of His gifts is to be an author; therefore, I write. You have to know yourself if you want to serve your partner and your household. There are other things that I am not so good at, which I work on as well to serve Kenady—for example, planning outings to hang out. Therefore, to serve her, I ask those around me, who are good at this, for ideas. But I know I can write a sweet note to top off the rendezvous and bring it all together for Kenady. Know what you are good at, and not so good at, in a relationship. It will reduce friction and limit your mistakes early on.

Know Whom You Are Serving

"For even the Son of Man came not to be served but to serve, and to give his life as a ransom for many" (Mark 10:45 ESV). When we were radio hosts, we had a great opportunity to serve our local community and bring in guests who are wonderful human beings. We know they have their struggles, but they are striving to live as Christ intended.

One of these individuals is Sylvia Broom. She works with an organization that helps the homeless here in Atlanta. She taught me something that changed my perspective on serving others. She said that when you serve people, it's not a zoo. When we stand behind tables, we never break our boundaries and really get to know the people we are serving. Therefore, her organization came up with more humane language: instead of saying they are "feeding the homeless," they choose to see their efforts as serving those who may have had some misfortune. They have also removed the barrier of the tables and now take the food directly to the people they serve, sitting down with them. They get to know the people on a first-name basis.

After this interview, I was motivated to be more personable with those who are in my community. I believe I can sometimes be so focused on getting the next project done that I don't think about serving my family and friends. I don't spend time trying to understand them on more than a superficial level. This reminds me of when, in

John 8, some scribes and Pharisees threw an adulterous woman on the ground in front of Jesus, because they wanted her to be punished for this particular sin. Jesus symbolically humbled Himself, kneeling down to talk to the women. He gave her respect even though she was guilty of sin. In such ways, He truly saw people whom everyone else had discounted.

We have the same opportunity. Listen, we *get* to respect people and serve them even though they might be the outcasts of society. We *get* to love people who do not look like us, believe in what we believe, or value the same things. We get to love and serve the way Jesus showed us.

Benevolent

> So husbands ought to love their own wives as their own bodies; he who loves his wife loves himself. For no one ever hated his own flesh, but nourishes and cherishes it, just as the Lord does the church.... Nevertheless let each one of you in particular so love his own wife as himself, and let the wife see that she respects her husband.
>
> —Ephesians 5:28–29, 33 (NKJV)

Loving your spouse doesn't start in marriage, but before. One thing that Kenady and I encourage singles to do is have roommates (of the same sex). Why? When you have roommates, they can be a mirror to some of your habits that can be worked on as you get to know yourself better. Also, roommates can help you exercise the muscle of benevolence. After all, regardless of what your future wife does, and whether she is cold or has mood swings or even rejects you in some way, you must love her. In this, you will model our Savior and what He did.

In 1 Corinthians, popularly known as the Love Chapter, verse 4 tells us that love or charity is both patient and kind. As men prepare to be husbands to beautiful wives, it is imperative to work on these attributes. I have figured out that I can be kind to Kenady anytime I want because it is a choice—and it is really not that hard, because she is kind to me. But I started being kind to my roommates before Kenady came along.

I want you to think about how you can be kind to your roommates and family members. If someone asks you to use your vehicle, what will you say? What happens when you see dirty dishes that you did not create in the sink? What should you do? Yell and curse out everybody in the house, or just do them and not say one word? What about writing an encouraging card for someone's birthday or another special occasion? These are just simple things you can start practicing now, before your future spouse comes along.

The funny thing is that some people might think I am a natural romantic after reading this section. I can tell you that's far from the truth, which is that before we got married, I could be emotionally unavailable due to my hesitation of getting too intimate with Kenady. I have had to walk intentionally in the Spirit, seeking counsel from God and my accountability for ideas on doing kind things for Kenady.

I also learned that it is impossible to truly care for Kenady in the way God intends unless I first love myself—which was sometimes as simple as taking myself out for dinner or a movie, or treating myself to my favorite eatery or ice cream/yogurt. It's hard to give what you don't have. Jesus indicated this when He told his followers, "And the second is like it: 'Love your neighbor as yourself'" (Matthew 22:39 NIV). Loving God is a strong indication that you love yourself. When you love God and yourself, you can't help but try to love others, and doing so will bring you much fulfillment.

Abide

In our twenty-first century, one of the phrases that has floated around the media and become extremely popular with the millennial generation is "stay woke." This generation is trying to urge others to be aware of what's really going on, instead of getting caught up in either media propaganda or conspiracy theories. My purpose is not to try to lead you down a rabbit hole of information on which, at best. I merely have an opinion, but to point out that the phrase "stay woke" can have a spiritual application. As men of God, many of us have been asleep, putting other things in place of what really matters, and it's time to wake up—to "get woke" and "stay woke."

Just look at Jesus in the Garden of Gethsemane. Matthew 26:40 says, "Then he returned to his disciples and found them sleeping: 'Couldn't you men keep watch with me for one hour?' he asked Peter" (NIV). Another word for keeping watch, used in other translations, is to tarry. Webster defines tarry as "to linger in expectation, wait and to abide or stay in or at a place."[22]

Too many men don't know how to abide, dwell, or tarry. There's an opportunity here for us as men of God. We are supposed to be abiding expectantly with our spouses, treating women how God intended, but instead, some of us are just planting seeds (having sex outside of marriage) and then leaving the nest. It's a horrible epidemic. God created the process of family, which we discussed already: we are to leave (our parents), cleave, and then weave. Too many men are trying to have sex (weave) and then leaving—and instead of leaving their parents, they are leaving their partners.

According to Lifeway Research Group, for men who attend Sunday school as an adult, there is a 55% chance their child will attend as well. However, for women, the result is only a 15% chance that the child will attend. And when a woman in a two-parent household gives her life to Christ, there is a 17% chance the children will follow her lead. However, when the father leads the way in this, there is a 93% probability everyone else in the household will follow.[23]

Men, you need to be present in the home. Our future depends on spiritually healthy families raising their children together. I am calling on all men to stand up, take responsibility, and take their rightful place in the home. Let's get our households in order. Men, let's till the ground, water, and fertilize the individuals in our home with the Word of God, raise our children so they can grow up properly, and manage the process of family headship God has instituted.

How do we accomplish this? We must learn how to abide in Christ. The symbolism on which we must draw is the vine and the branch metaphor. In John 15:5–8, Jesus explained:

> I am the vine; you are the branches. If you remain in me and I in you, you will bear much fruit; apart from me you can do nothing. If you do not remain in me, you are like a branch that is thrown away and withers; such branches are picked up, thrown into the fire and burned. If you remain in me and my words remain in you, ask whatever you wish, and it will be done for you. This is to my Father's glory, that you bear much fruit, showing yourselves to be my disciples. (NIV)

You must learn how to make Jesus your number-one source of nourishment. I know there are plenty of things vying for your attention, but as Jesus said, without Him, "you can do nothing." He gives you the ability to have life, but He also wants you to know that if you want real significance in this world, you need His help. You must rest in the fact that He will never try to harm you. You should drink of His well, by receiving the Holy Spirit, and eat His food, which is His word. You must learn to abide, waiting in expectation and trusting that He wants to supply all of your needs, and believe that He who started a good work in you will complete it.

To conclude, abiding in Christ gives you access to the fruit of the Spirit. Self-control as well as patience is needed to navigate through this world and your relationship with your spouse. You will potentially be married (if you aren't already) and practicing self-control, which is vital for your success, significance, and spiritual maturity. Self-control leads us back to living upright and holy lives for Christ.

So "staying woke" is more than a phrase. It's a lifestyle!

New

Ephesians 5:26–27 says: "…to make her holy, cleansing her by the washing with water through the word, and to present her to himself as a radiant church, without stain or wrinkle or any other blemish, but holy and blameless" (NIV). To be able to wash your wife with the Word of God, you as a husband should already know Scripture and be applying it to your own life. The men have to be, as Jesus told Nicodemus in John 3, born again. This is a spiritual birth, or rebirth, in which you are born of the spirit. It's a spiritual regeneration.

Paul directs us, in 2 Corinthians 5:17 (KJV), "Therefore if any man be in Christ, he is a *new creature*: old things are passed away; behold, all things are become new" (emphasis added). Are you renewed? Have you surrendered your life to Christ? It doesn't matter how established in this earth you are financially, politically, or socially. Without being a new person, you can have a lot of success, but in heaven, your works outside of God will be treated like paper ready for a bonfire.

By confessing you are sinner—falling short of what God expects—and repenting or turning away from your old ways, believing God raised Jesus from the grave for your sake, you will be made new. Then you can begin cleansing your wife in earnest. However, you don't have to wait until marriage to start planting seeds! Even before we were married, I would share Scripture with Kenady, practicing for marriage. When you do this, then when life comes at you hard, you both have a stronger foundation to fall upon than just your natural talent to lead or manage.

Becoming new includes intentionally closing the doors on past relationships. Remember, there's no plan B. There is no other option. Relationship takes a lot of work, so even if it were permissible, why would you add the burden of maintaining communication with multiple women? To do so is immaturity and insecurity, regardless of whether or not your partner is currently satisfying all of your needs or expectations of her. Besides, you will never be fully satisfied by any person, even your spouse. If you try, there will always be an emptiness and broken places inside of you that Jesus with His Holy Spirit is yearning to fill. He desires you to be new, renewed by His Holy Spirit and His word, especially in marriage as you serve your wife and family.

Dedicated

This word is so important: it's one thing to abide in our relationships, but it's another when we are dedicated to the cause. There have been many men who stayed around physically but without being present at all spiritually or emotionally. Dedication speaks to the purpose of the relationship because the dedicated man has asked himself, "Why am I here?" and answers his own question by showing up each and every day for his wife and children. He is dedicated to providing and being generous for his family.

A dedicated man is also a defender of the faith. He makes sure that His children are trained in the way they should go. He does his best to present godly behavior so his kids can have the best picture of what a man looks like.

Dedication and faithfulness run all through the Bible. Abraham was the father of faith, who took his son to the mountain to sacrifice him. Elisha was faithful to Elijah as Elijah transitioned from this earth to heaven. Daniel was faithful to God, as he did not bow his knee to any other gods. Joseph (Jesus' father) was faithful to Mary even though Jesus was not conceived by him. And most importantly, Jesus was faithful to God's purpose as He willingly laid down His life for you and me. God is looking for you to take a stand, to be committed to Him and to your family regardless of what the world is currently doing.

Finally, dedication speaks to being dependable. Yes, your trust should be in God alone, but you represent God by keeping your word. If you can't do it, do not commit to things that God has not given you grace to do. Whatever you try to do with your own power, God may allow you to sustain by yourself, but if God has started something, He can be depended on completely to sustain it *for* you. Grace doesn't just speak to the unmerited or undeserved favor of God but also means an undeserved ability to do the things He intends. If God has called you into marriage, believe me, He has supernatural grace for you, to enable you to be dependable for your family!

As a man previously preparing to be a husband, and as a man married several months at the time of writing, I truly believe that these keys will help establish a firm foundation in a man's life. If a man honestly desires to be the Kingdom husband God has called him to be, he will take the necessary steps to develop the qualities listed above. Also, familiarity with these principles will help women know how to spot a godly man or encourage their current partner in godly directions. Of course, above all, the Bible has to be the central focus of the man's life as he strives to build a devotional life, which will help him lead his future family. But the seven biblically-based principles in this chapter are useful as practical starting points or points of reference.

#COMPLETELYMARRIED

Chapter 13:
How to Prepare to Be a Wife

Almost every woman has dreamed of becoming married and having her dream wedding, especially when she was young. Many of us grow up with fantasy romance stories featuring a glamorized princess finding her Prince Charming and living happily ever after in a big, beautiful castle. I (Kenady) know I'm guilty of idolizing this depiction of true love and fairytale weddings. I had even picked out my wedding dress, wedding ring, dream venue, and color scheme all by the age of 18.

We often prepare for our wedding day but don't usually prepare for the time after our wedding. Although there is nothing wrong with planning for our special day, it would be wise to also prepare for becoming a wife. The wedding lasts only for a few hours while being a wife will last until death do you part.

In order to prepare to be a wife, one must understand God's intentions for creating Eve, the first wife. A wife was made to be a helper for her husband. In Genesis 2:18 (ESV) it says: "Then the LORD God said, 'It is not good for the man to be alone. I will make a *helper* who is just right for him'" (emphasis added).

The word *helper* isn't usually a term that brings great joy and excitement. It is often looked at negatively, as if referring to a slave or someone else in an inferior position. However, the Holy Spirit is referred to as "the Helper" in John 14:26 (ESV, NIV). Thus, I can assure you, being a helper represents a high honor in God's eyes. We should no longer show contempt at being a helper but should take this role seriously. I have created a mnemonic device using HELPER that will lay out certain qualities we as women can develop as we prepare to become a wife.

Humble Submission

Ever since the fall of man in the Garden, there has been a power struggle between husband and wife (see Genesis 3:16). Due to sin entering into the world through the disobedience of Adam (and Eve), most women have a sin-nature to be strong-willed and want to usurp the headship of their husbands. Consequently, men try to force their leadership and power over their wives. But thank God, we do not have to be subjected to our sin nature! As we become born again, we can live the life that God originally intended for us to live—one of unity and harmony between husband and wife.

If I could guess, submission is probably one of the top three most hated words for Christian women. I think this is mainly because we often have a misunderstanding and poor example of what true submission looks like. Submission is often seen as a state of weakness, silence, and being controlled. This, however, is far from the truth. It takes true strength to humble oneself and submit in any situation, especially marriage.

To me, submission is getting behind or supporting a vision or a mission. It is vitally important to make sure the man you are marrying is someone you can trust and whose leading you can follow. You must believe in the mission God has given him for the family. If you are skeptical of his ability to lead, then it would probably be best to evaluate your relationship with him before you make the commitment of "I do." If his mission is only to fulfill his wants and desires, then you might not want to agree to get on that boat. We get to choose our head. In Western culture, we aren't forced or arranged into marriage like back in the day.

Submission has often been viewed in a negative light because leadership has frequently been abused. As a result, submission is sometimes looked at as a way to tame women and put us in a cage. Some men have spewed out this word as a way to get us to do what they say. A true man of God should know that being appointed as the head comes with major responsibilities, as Damien wrote about in the previous chapter. It doesn't mean a man sits on his throne with his feet up, demanding his wife to feed him grapes. No, being the head and leader means a man has a special responsibility to serve in the kingdom of God and is held to a higher standard by Him. That is why God approached Adam first in the garden after they sinned.

I believe God is bringing back order in the way marriages function, by raising up godly men and godly women who understand what headship and submission mean. After all, we are all called to submit "to one another out of reverence for Christ" (Ephesians 5:21 ESV).
I think of submitting as getting under your husband's umbrella in the rain. There's only room for one to hold the umbrella. You have to stoop low (humility) to get underneath his covering, and you must follow his lead or you will step out of the umbrella and get wet. Pride says, "I don't need your umbrella, I have my own," or "I'd rather get wet." Humble submission says, "I will join you by stepping under your protection, follow your leading, and trusting that you will get us

safely to where we need to be." It doesn't mean that you aren't capable of holding the umbrella or leading, but it's better to be under the same umbrella or mission in order to have closeness and intimacy, and to walk in unity. A wise husband will communicate and partner with his wife because she has different strengths, experiences, viewpoints, and thinking than he does. She has value and gifts God has given her that should not be silenced or brushed to the side.

I remember one Saturday evening, Damien and I were walking from the car parking lot across the street to the church doors. We were joking around about something, and Damien stopped walking to see if I would follow his lead and stop as well. I purposefully continued to walk ahead and even strutted down the sidewalk ahead of him as if it were a runway. There were these two men driving past us in a pickup truck. One of the men popped his head out of the truck, whistling, and yelled, "You looking good ma, I see you!" I immediately gasped, turned around in embarrassment, and ran back to Damien. Because I was away from his covering and protection, those guys did not realize that I was taken. Quite frankly, in that moment, I did not act like I was, either. Though we were able to joke about it afterward, this incident reveals what happens too often in marriages and relationships. We as women tend to walk ahead and not beside our men, yielding to their leadership. Thus, due to not submitting to our husband's leading, we can open up room for attacks in our lives and in our marriages from outside sources.

I have to be honest: submission does not come naturally to me. My flesh wants to rebel and do things my own way. It is something that I have to be intentional with and continue to work on. If you have a hard time with the concept of submitting, then look to Jesus, our great example. He lived a life of humility and complete submission unto God the Father, and He was far from weak. Philippians 2:8–9 reads,

"He humbled himself by becoming obedient to death—even death on a cross! Therefore God exalted him to the highest place and gave him the name that is above every name" (NIV). He was far greater than the power of death but submitted Himself for a greater good, and that greater good was to save us. As a reward, He was given the highest place of honor and is waiting for us as His ultimate bride.

We, as women, have the opportunity to submit to our husbands. It is not that we are not capable of leading, but it is for a bigger purpose and greater good that we submit. That good is to show the world what it looks like to be submitted unto God. As we were made in the image of God, to reflect Him, marriage is a reflection of Christ and the Church. Ephesians 5:22–24 says, "Wives, submit yourselves to your own husbands as you do to the Lord. For the husband is the head of the wife as Christ is the head of the church, his body, of which he is the Savior. Now as the church submits to Christ, so also wives should submit to their husbands in everything" (NIV).

Submission is such a beautiful thing. Like Jesus, we will be rewarded for our humility. We will be able to draw people to Jesus as well as see blessings flow in our marriages. How can we proclaim to be Christians but not live a life submitted to our husbands the way we submit to God? We are no different than the world if we walk in pride and high regard for ourselves. Instead, we get to be a light in the way we carry ourselves in marriage, with meekness and gentleness. We don't submit with a grudge, or forcefully, but should submit voluntarily. This shows that we respect our husbands and the authority God has given them. When we respect men, we show that we love and honor them.

You don't have to wait until you are married to practice submission and humility. In what areas in your life can you practice humility and submission? Is it at your job, by submitting to the authority of your boss? What about at home, where you can serve your family or roommates? We are all called to live a life of humility and submission, not only as wives and in marriage but also with God and other fellow believers. It is a quality you can sharpen wherever you are.

Equal

As a result of the fall of man in the Garden of Eden, women have been looked down upon, mistreated, and seen as inferior to men. We have seen it play out all over the world, throughout history, even still to this day. However, because of the death and resurrection of Jesus Christ almost two thousand years ago, He has redeemed and restored us back to the original state of equality.

Galatians 3:28 says, "There is neither Jew nor Greek, there is neither slave nor free, there is no male and female, for you are all one in Christ Jesus" (ESV). We as believers need to let this become our reality, in our lives and in our marriages. We are all one. There is no difference in value between men and women. The wife is not less than her husband—and she is not greater than him, either.

Unfortunately, in the world, we see people act otherwise. In some cases, there continues to be oppression of women, while in other cases we see the idolization of women. There is a movement trying to elevate women while devaluing men. If you consider yourself to be a disciple of Jesus Christ, you cannot be a part of any of this. Yes, it is important to fight for the rights of the oppressed, but not at the expense of others. We need to see our brothers as well as our sisters in Christ as equals. We need to honor the men in our lives, even before marriage. Don't think that when you get married you will suddenly be able to respect a man if you're accustomed to acting otherwise.

Equality means having the same value, but it does not indicate the same position. In a marriage, a husband and a wife have different roles to play. Just like with any team, all players are vital. If a player is missing or not doing his or her part, the whole team is affected. When all team members are in position and giving it their all, the whole team is bound to succeed. They should work together, knowing each other's strengths and weaknesses. Encourage one another and help one another! There should not be any competition among players on the same team. In marriage, Christ is the Most Valuable Player, anyways. When He is on your team and in your marriage, everyone wins. So as you prepare to be a helper and a wife, you must understand the concept of equality between husband and wife so that you will not seek to be in opposition to your partner. Recognizing that this is a move in position and not value will also make it easier to submit.

Loving

When I was writing this section of the chapter, oddly enough, I found it was the most difficult part for me. I'm sure it is no surprise, as you are preparing to become a wife and a helper, that you must learn to be loving to your husband. After all, as Christians we are all called to love everyone. It would have been easy for me to write about the romantic side of love, for anyone who knows me knows that I have a big heart and love hard. I am a hopeless romantic, or a sap you might say. I just *love* love. The mushy, tear-jerking love stories—I'm here for it all. Based on *The Five Love Languages* by Gary Chapman, my top love languages (aside from food!) are quality time and touch, though due to the boundaries Damien and I set before marriage, we didn't do the touchy-feely stuff.

However, as I sought God to see what He wanted me to write about regarding love, I felt He didn't want me to write about how to love in that way. I believe He wanted me to talk about committed or steadfast love—a love that is not based on feelings, emotions, or circumstances, but a love that is based off of making a decision. According to Merriam-Webster, *steadfast* means to be "firmly fixed in place, immovable, not subject to change."[24] We all know that emotions are not fixed; they are very movable and are likely to change depending on your mood, your hormones, or if you're like me, based on your level of hunger.

The Bible talks a lot about God's steadfast love for us. Lamentations 3:22 says, "The steadfast love of the LORD never ceases; his mercies never come to an end" (ESV). Likewise, Psalm 118:1 says, "Oh give thanks to the LORD, for he is good; for his steadfast love endures forever!" (ESV). Praise God that He has made a choice to love us in spite of ourselves, because we can be some shady, wishy-washy, idolizing individuals!

In the famous Love Chapter, chapter 13 of 1 Corinthians, verses 5 and 7 say in part, "It is not irritable, and it keeps no record of being wronged. ... Love never gives up, never loses faith, is always hopeful, and endures through every circumstance" (NLT).

So, how do we have a steadfast love that is enduring, that isn't moody, that doesn't keep tallies, and that never loses faith? We must learn the art of forgiveness and mercy. Damien and I made a practice of this in our courtship. We were quick to communicate offenses, to admit our wrongdoings, to ask for forgiveness and to forgive each other. This helps us to learn from our mistakes, grow in our love, and not let the enemy get between us. Communication is key, but remaining humble to allow the Holy Spirit to keep you in check is a *major* key.

I remember one night Damien and I were on the phone and I got caught up in my feelings. I told him I was going to hang up and then hung up on him. (Side note: it's rude to hang up on someone even if you give him or her advance notice.) I was then trying to go to sleep, but the Holy Spirit would not let me. I ended up calling him back about fifteen minutes later to apologize, and Damien forgave me. He then said, jokingly, "You're so in love with me, you couldn't even go to sleep without apologizing." He may or may not have been right.

Proverbs 17:9 says, "Love prospers when a fault is forgiven, but dwelling on it separates close friends" (NLT). Our love and respect for each other grew even more after overcoming that fault and our many other past faults. We grew closer instead of apart. I had to set my pride and feelings aside and call him back because I did not want both of us to feel a certain type of way and go to bed in that state. I definitely didn't want to let the enemy plant any bad seeds in either of our minds or hearts.

This wasn't the first time, and will definitely not be the last time, we have to forgive one another. Neither one of us is perfect, and we both know that, so we have to make room for each other's wrongdoings because we are human: "Make allowance for each other's faults, and forgive anyone who offends you. Remember, the Lord forgave you, so you must forgive others" (Colossians 3:13 NLT). This doesn't mean we abuse each other by wronging them, but it gives us a heads up that because we are both sinners, we are going to sin. Thus, we have to learn to forgive. I don't intentionally hurt Damien, and neither does he hurt me on purpose, but it happens. Our love for each other allows us to get past those transgressions. First Peter 4:8 tells us to "continue to show deep love for each other, for love covers a multitude of sins" (NLT). Proverbs 10:12 says, "Hatred stirs up quarrels, but love makes up for all offenses" (NLT). Love is a way we can overcome the sins of one another. Forgiveness gives us an opportunity to let the roots of our love grow stronger and deeper and remain immovable. Bitterness and unforgiveness that go unchecked, however, can slowly pull up the roots of love, ultimately breaking up relationships and, unfortunately, marriages. We pray that this will not be the case for anyone reading this.

It is inevitable that as a helper and a wife, you are going to get upset about something your spouse will do or say, and vice versa, but you have to choose to forgive and to remain steadfast in your love in order to remain by his side. Thank God that He doesn't give up on us! This should be our motivation to show the same committed love and mercy to our spouses: because we are going to need it from them, from others, and from God.

Prayer Warrior

When me and Damien were taking Pre-Married Life, a premarital class provided through Victory World Church, our facilitators asked us about our expectations and desired qualities for our spouse. Among other things, I mentioned Damien handling all car issues. I am guilty of being the girl who will drive a car until the wheels fall off, to avoid potentially being taken advantage of at a car shop due to my naivety regarding all things car-related.

Damien, on the other hand, mentioned a profound quality that he wanted in his wife. He stated he wanted someone who will also pray and war for the family in the Spirit. This definitely caught everyone in our group's attention.

Oftentimes we think men are the only ones who should pray over the family and household. Yes, they should be the spiritual leaders, but they should not be warring alone: "A person standing alone can be attacked and defeated, but two can stand back-to-back and conquer. Three are even better, for a triple-braided cord is not easily broken" (Ecclesiastes 4:12 NLT).

We need to stand together with our husbands, attacking the enemy and praying forth the Word of God over our families. There is no better way to fight than in prayer. It's an even better fight when you pray together, in accord, men and women alike. Acts 1:14 says, "All these with one accord were devoting themselves to prayer, together with the women and Mary the mother of Jesus, and his brother" (ESV).

Those who are familiar with the book of Acts know that there are countless stories of salvations, healings, and great wonders and miracles that took place. This happened due to unity, prayer, and the power of the Holy Spirit. These same things *should* be happening in our lives, our marriages, our families, and our communities today. We need to be women who seek God in prayer for breakthrough. I know I have often been guilty of not being consistent in my prayer life, but in preparing to become a wife to Damien and hopefully, one day, to become a mother, I have tried to be intentional with sharpening this aspect of my life. I have realized the importance of being a woman who prays.

In the Bible, we see several women who accomplished much through their prayers. Hannah prayed for a son and promised to dedicate him to God (1 Samuel 1:10–11). We know, then, that we can be women who pray for our children and that they will be devoted to serving God. Esther sought God through prayer and fasting to find favor with the king to save her people (Esther 4:15–17). Likewise, we can stand boldly in front of our King for our community and the oppression of others. Anna was a widow who devoted herself to prayer and prophesied the coming of Jesus the Messiah (Luke 2:36–38). In the same manner, we can pray for unbelievers to come to the knowledge of Jesus Christ before His second coming.

We as women also have the responsibility to take dominion in the earth. As prayer warriors, we must "put on the full armor of God" so we can stand against the schemes of the enemy, as it says in Ephesians 6:11 (NIV). When we are fully armored, our assignment is to "pray in the Spirit on all occasions with all kinds of prayers and requests. With this in mind, be alert and always keep on praying for all the Lord's people" (Ephesians 6:18 NIV). Ladies, the beauty of this is that we are all commanded to be prayer warriors regardless of our gender or relationship status. So whether you are single, engaged, married, or widowed, let's be warring women who pray down heaven with prayers of faith, standing in full confidence that God hears and will answer them.

Encouraging

As a young girl, I played several sports, one of them being cheerleading. And yes, cheerleading is a sport. It is not up for debate. I remember there were quite a few times where I had to cheer in all types of weather conditions—in the cold, in the blistering heat, and even in the rain during football season. Regardless of the weather or the score, it was our role to cheer the boys on. We were expected to show enthusiasm, even if they were down by thirty points in thirty-degree weather. In the same manner, as wives, we get to be our husband's biggest cheerleader and number one fan, for better or for worse, during sunny days or rainy days.

We get to be in their corner during this boxing match called life. They are constantly taking blows from life, other people, the media, the enemy, and even themselves. It's not to say that we as women don't get attacked as well or that men aren't to encourage us in return. However, the enemy attacks the head the hardest because when the head is gone, the body cannot function. We need to encourage him with our words and not continue to knock him down. We can see from a different vantage point and give him insight. We need to build up our head and not continue to bring him down when the world around him is already doing that. There is nothing worse for him than coming home after a long day amid words of death and continuing to receive more of the same from his wife.

Your husband should be able to confide in you and be vulnerable with you without fear of you saying, "I told you so," "You ain't a man," "You are just like your father," etc. If you are nagging or attacking him and never uplifting him, he will likely seek other sources of comfort. We must learn to lift him up despite our feelings or what we are going through. We should be the reassuring voice that encourages our man to continue to keep pushing, to follow the ways of the Lord, and to do what God is calling him to do.

Job 2:7–9 says, "So Satan left the LORD's presence, and he struck Job with terrible boils from head to foot. Job scraped his skin with a piece of broken pottery as he sat among the ashes. His wife said to him, 'Are you still trying to maintain your integrity? Curse God and die'" (NLT).

Here we see Job's wife dropped the ball in the area of encouragement. But just like her, we are flawed human beings. We can't get mad and judge her for her words. Job's wife had also lost her children and her wealth. She was going through a season of loss, just like him. However, your circumstances don't excuse you to speak death. You can be intentional to always sow words of encouragement and not let your emotions or your current season get in the way.

When you are challenged with the role of encourager, you have to address the areas in your heart that might harbor bitterness. Bitterness can interfere with your ability to truly encourage your husband in seasons when money is tight, people have turned their back on you, or sickness or death have come near your loved ones. It's easy to be hostile with your words during trying times, but if you are intentional to speak life, it will benefit not only your husband but also you and your household.

We women have the power to set the atmosphere in our homes. We can make it either peaceful or chaotic. Proverbs 21:19 says, "It is better to live in a desert than with a quarrelsome and nagging wife" (NIV), while Proverbs 14:1 observes, "A wise woman builds her home, but a foolish woman tears it down with her own hands" (NLT).

Let's learn to be wise women and make a practice of being an encourager, not just to our men, but also to the people around us. This world can use more of this.

Righteous

One of the most important qualities a woman should have as she is preparing to become a wife is righteousness. I don't mean righteous as in doing right or living right—though I am not saying you aren't to live holy and submit to God's commands. Nor am I referring to what we so commonly hear as the Proverbs 31 woman, who appears to be this perfect, virtuous woman who can do many wonderful things. Fixation on this standard can make you look at your life and skill set and feel less than or incapable of ever living up to expectations. Don't get me wrong: I am not coming against striving to be a stronger woman of God who makes a huge impact on those around her. Nevertheless, the true righteousness to which I am referring is the righteousness found only in Christ Jesus.

I am looking at righteousness through the lens of *justification*. Justification means that something is right or righteous in the sight of God. Therefore, by righteous, I mean someone who has been made right with God. It is only Jesus who can make us righteous, not any religious acts or living a good ole "Christian life."

In order to be a godly wife and the true helper that the Lord intends for you to be, you must accept Jesus Christ as your Lord and Savior. It is through Him that you have the power to overcome sin and the fallen, evil nature we all share, by the power of the Holy Spirit. How can you truly help someone if your soul, your body, and your spirit are unredeemed, helpless, and hopeless? You have to be helping from the side of righteousness, or else you could be influencing your husband in the wrong way.

Jezebel is a clear biblical example of "helping" from the side of unrighteousness. She was a wicked wife, who did not have faith in the Lord and was not submitted to His laws and decrees. She manipulated and controlled her husband, King Ahab, and often took matters into her own hands. She brought him harm and not good. But we are different. We are women of righteousness, who have been redeemed and washed in the blood of Jesus Christ and are in the proper stance to help.

As women of righteousness, we are new and are free from the sin/guilt of our past. Second Corinthians 5:17 says, "This means that anyone who belongs to Christ has become a new person. The old life is gone; a new life has begun!" (NLT). As mentioned earlier in this book, Damien did not have sex before marriage. However, that was not the case for me. Now, I could either be ashamed of not being married as a virgin, wallowing in my past and forever living with guilt and shame, or I could receive with gladness the redemption and new life that have been given to me through repentance and faith in Jesus. I don't know your story, but whatever it is, you do not have to be ashamed of it! Nothing you have done is too powerful for the blood of Jesus to overcome. It was finished at the cross. You do not have to hold on to any guilt or shame. Repent, turn to God, and give Him your messy past.

As women of righteousness, we have power over sin. The book of Romans says, "We know that our old sinful selves were crucified with Christ so that sin might lose its power in our lives. We are no longer slaves to sin. For when we died with Christ we were set free from the power of sin. … Do not let sin control the way you live; do not give in to sinful desires. Do not let any part of your body become an instrument of evil to serve sin. Instead, give yourselves completely to God, for you were dead, but now you have new life. So use your whole body as an instrument to do what is right for the glory of God" (Romans 6:6–7 and 12–13 NLT).

The power of sin is broken due to what Jesus did on the cross. You are no longer hopeless and controlled by sin. You have the power to overcome sexual immorality, lying, gossip, pride, greed, and all the rest. I'm not saying you will never sin, but you will no longer make a practice of it or be ruled by it. By the grace of God, you have everything you need to live in obedience to Him—because "God is working in you, giving you the desire and the power to do what pleases him" (Philippians 2:13 NLT).

As women of righteousness, we have confidence. If I can be completely honest, I have struggled somewhat with confidence in becoming the wife that Damien needs. Maybe you, too, have wondered, "Am I strong enough? Will I be able to add value into his life? Will I be a good wife?" The answer is, through the grace and power of God, yes! You are not in this alone. God will give you the wisdom, grace, and strength to be the helper your husband needs. And thankfully, you are not taking the place of God in his life.

So take the pressure off of yourself. You can come boldly to God with confidence in whatever you need, including in regard to your husband. First John 3:21–22 says, "Dear friends, if we don't feel guilty, we can come to God with bold confidence. And we will receive from him whatever we ask because we obey him and do the things that please him" (NLT). If you feel like you need more patience for your husband, more love for him, or more wisdom regarding him, ask God with confidence, knowing that He will give it to you. If you can have confidence before the great Almighty God as his daughter, you can stand confidently at your husband's side as his helper and wife.

Bonus Nugget

As a Registered Dietitian, I couldn't end this chapter without mentioning the need to also prepare your body to be a mother. I know, most people don't want to even think about having kids within the first few years of being married. However, the truth of the matter is, though you may have your plans, it's the Lord's plans that supersede your own. Proverbs 19:21 says, "You can make many plans, but the LORD's purpose will prevail" (NLT). God has the power to open and close the womb and the sovereign will to bring forth whatever is necessary for His purpose at whatever time He sees fit. No birth control or fertility tracker can stop Him! I know several people who have gotten pregnant within the first year of marriage, or even had a honeymoon baby, without planning. Once you say, "I do," and start "doing the do" (because I know you are abstaining from sex until marriage as you're reading this, right?), you can very well become pregnant. That's how God created it to work, so it only makes sense to start preparing now.

Before you get married, you need to get your body into shape. You have to prepare healthy soil (your body) to nourish a seed (a growing baby). Generally speaking, this means eating healthier, such as consuming more whole grains, fruits, veggies, nuts, and seeds, cooking more at home, and drinking more water. It's also important to become moderately active (if you aren't already), take care of your mental health, and take a multivitamin so you aren't deficient in any nutrient. *(Make sure to consult with your doctor before making any of these health changes previously mentioned.)* Conception is such a crucial point because a baby's nervous system is forming before a mom even knows she's pregnant. You want to give your baby the best start, of course—and as with your marriage as a whole, that starts now.

Part 4:
To the Altar and Beyond

#COMPLETELYMARRIED

Chapter 14:
Planning Your Wedding

So, how do you plan for the wedding? What things do you need to consider in setting up your registry? Though this chapter is not the last say on wedding planning, or a complete list of everything you should know or need to do, we want to share our mindset and experience regarding wedding planning in hopes that you can glean some useful information.

Before we start, we will say that wedding planning can be stressful if you let it be—and even if you don't, it can still be a lot to handle. Try to filter everything through peace, grace, and vision. You will have to make a lot of decisions and work together with your future spouse. It will be a great exercise in compromising, sacrificing, and submitting. Take it in stride. Spread tasks out and get help from others so you don't lose your mind and suffer through your engagement season due to the struggles of wedding planning. Remember, you are a bride/groom for one day, but you will be a wife/husband until death do you part. The most important thing isn't *getting* married but the foundation you have built to *stay* married.

DAMIEN K. H. NASH AND KENADY NASH

First, we sat down and planned everything out. Fortunately, we'd been to several weddings, and I (Damien) had personally experienced weddings from the "inside," whether as a groomsman or best man. For our wedding, our focus was always on *purpose*, so we wanted to budget everything out. Budgets are essential for every aspect of your relationship, so as we prepared to come together, we felt it was important to make one. We kept in mind that we had other expenses in the future, beyond the wedding, like a home, starting our business, getting out of debt, etc. So even if you have $10,000, that doesn't mean you should spend all of it on the wedding, and you definitely don't want to go into *more* debt as you begin your life together in marriage. Stay realistic with your budget and figure out if other people, like parents, will be contributing. Unexpected expenses will most likely arise, but you should try your best to stay within budget. Taking from other areas of the wedding budget to cover those additional costs would be wiser than constantly increasing your limit.

You may be someone who wants to stay true to wedding etiquette and follow all of the conventional "rules" to a T. However, that was not the case for us. As part of staying in budget, we chose not to send hard-copy invitations but used electronic versions instead. We bargained and found great deals on our venue and food. We were also blessed to have friends and family help in other capacities. If possible, see if people you know can help with particular tasks to make your wedding more cost-effective. Do you have someone who can make your flowers, as an alternative to an expensive florist? Do you have a friend who is gifted in planning and would love to help coordinate your wedding? If so, use those resources! The key thing, though, is that the people who help should be *gifted* in those areas. We understand the expression "you get what you pay for," but your wedding can still have quality when you use people who are skilled in these areas. Don't forget to honor them with a gift or a small token of your appreciation, in turn, in whatever way you are able.

One of the most important things to remember when planning and staying in budget is not to people please. People pleasing is expensive. You worry about having the best food, the best venue, the best, the best, the best—when in reality, the people you want at your wedding shouldn't care about those things. They should be there to celebrate your union out of love for you and your future spouse. Don't waste money on people who just want to find something wrong with your special day. Keep that in mind when creating your guest list. I'm sure there are a ton of people you would love to invite, yet you have to keep the volume realistic to what you can afford. People may be offended, but they should understand. We were unable to invite every single person we wanted at the wedding because we were passionate about staying in our lane and within our means.

Another tip we noticed as we were planning: wedding season is real. This usually falls between the months of April/May and September/October. Everything is usually more expensive during these months, especially in the summer, because that's when most people are getting married. We were planning our wedding for over nine months. When we scoped out different prices on various things well in advance, we noticed prices ended up almost doubling if we waited to buy it closer to our wedding date. So when you can, get things as early as possible and outside of wedding season. Also keep in mind that getting married on a Friday or Sunday is usually cheaper. We got married on a Sunday for a more affordable price. On the other hand, some places, like table and chair rentals, are closed on Sundays, so plan in advance to work around those sorts of roadblocks.

Below are some other wedding details to keep in mind when planning. This is not an exhaustive list. It might be helpful to find a full wedding planning list at a wedding website like Zola, the Knot, or Wedding Wire, or you can buy a hard copy at a store. When reviewing the different items that require budget, choose the ones that are most important to you and rank them. Then plan to spend relatively more on the things that mean the most to you, while cutting corners on your lower priorities, to have a great wedding that remains within your budget.

- Theme of the wedding
- Wedding venue
- Wedding planner
- Day-of coordinator
- Invitations
- Rehearsal dinner
- Transportation for the bride and groom to/from the wedding
- Bridal party (bridesmaids and groomsmen)
- Bride's wedding dress
- Bridesmaid dresses
- Groom's tux
- Groomsmen tuxes (can include ring bearer and father of the bride)
- Music for wedding (live singers/musicians, or via CD or mp3)
- Decorations/flowers
- Pastor(s)
- Flower girl (typically, age 3–7)
- Ring bearer (typically, age 3–7)
- Photographer and/or videographer
- DJ/entertainment for reception
- Food and beverages
- Cake/desserts
- Favors and gifts for guests, bridal parties, ushers, etc.
- Honeymoon

We highly recommend a coordinator to help with the wedding. This person should have a gift for putting events together and organizing. Creativity is a plus. This position definitely reduces stress for everyone involved, especially the bride and groom—even more so if neither of them has a gift for administration or coordination.

It's so important for you and your spouse-to-be to maintain a vision and to have purposes that align. Our purpose as a couple, we realized, is to teach people how to live healthy, spiritually and physically, by watching what we partake in. When it came to the registry, we wanted to focus on coming together in terms of our ministry and business. Accordingly, we included electronics and cookware for our business on our registry. Yes, towels and décor are useful, but we challenge you to think also about things you can use to help with your future and your passions. This may lead you to ask for a particular software package or piece of equipment, for contributions to a charity, or for help sending one of you back to school. Don't limit your registry to items you could easily afford or might prefer to pick out yourself; think about your future and where God is leading you. Technology can be useful in facilitating financial gifts: you can use Cash App, Google Pay, PayPal, GoFundMe, Zelle, Venmo, or Square to fund your foundation, ministry, and future. Any extra cash can be used to pay down debt as well. The Knot.com, Mywedding.com, WeddingWire.com, and Zola.com are great resources to use in setting up wedding websites and registries.

It is important to discuss your plans for your honeymoon, too, so you're both on the same page. We felt like it was important for us to have our honeymoon directly after our wedding. Some people are not able to do this, so they plan on having it at a future date or go on a smaller trip. Be realistic: again, we suggest never going into more debt for any aspect of your wedding, including the honeymoon. You can also add it to your registry so other people can contribute.

Finally, don't forget that you have to apply for your marriage license in advance—possibly a couple of weeks before getting married. You can do this by going to the office of the county clerk or clerk of the court, depending on where you live. Though you should look up the specific requirements and procedures on your county website, expect that you will both need to be present to sign the appropriate documents when initially applying. Just in case, we recommend bringing two forms of ID, whether your state driver's license, SSN card, birth certificate, or passport. You should also be prepared with personal information like your city and state of birth, as well as certain details about your parents or guardians (e.g., legal names, birthplaces). The fee varies by state or locality, but we brought documentation of our premarital counseling class and received $40 off of our application fee.

Of course, don't forget to bring the paperwork to your wedding so that the pastor/minister or other licensed officiate can sign it immediately after the ceremony. Equally important is returning it to the clerk's office afterward. In some cases, this may be the responsibility of the officiate, but regardless, make sure it doesn't slip through the cracks! Then be on the lookout for the arrival of your marriage certificate.

The wedding process can be very hectic, we know. However, duly considering your own gifts and the gifts of those in your immediate circle, like family members and friends, can definitely lessen the burden. We also hope and pray that you don't rush to the altar and that you take our advice to budget so you will have a wedding within your means. Following this advice saved us a lot of heartache and gave us a lot of peace.

Chapter 15:
Wedding Day

The wedding day is supposed to be a celebration of three becoming one. We say three because in most modern weddings, couples are trying to leave God out of the mix. God is and will continue to be at the center of our lives.

The first wedding (union) was recorded in Genesis 2:18–25. God brought Eve in front of Adam, and they became one flesh. This was God's original intent for a man and a woman to get married; however, humans wanted to add to what God created. Throughout history, customary practices have changed on who should marry—including, in some cases, children marrying each other or adults, brothers marrying sisters, or especially nowadays, men marrying men and women marrying women. We implore you to study the Word of God for the truth about God's original intentions for marriage.

However, some of the human traditions, customs, and symbols that have arisen around marriage are not incompatible with the Word of God. Some of the following biblical and historical customs may seem familiar, others less so:

DAMIEN K. H. NASH and KENADY NASH

- The bride and bridegroom leave their respective chambers (see Joel 2:16).

- "…a bridegroom decks himself with a garland, and … a bride adorns herself with jewels." (Isaiah 61:10 NRSV)

- One should not mourn or fast on wedding day (see Matthew 9:15).

- Music and dancing are important features of the wedding feast (see Jeremiah 7:34).

- Special songs are sung for a wedding (see Psalm 78:63).

- Food and appropriate attire are important aspects of a wedding (see Matthew 22:1–14, Luke 14:7–24).

- Invitations are given for the wedding feast/banquet (see Matthew 22:1–14).

- Wine can sometimes be a celebratory drink offered and poured at the wedding (see John 2:1–11).

- Consummation (sign of a covenant) on the wedding night was seen as a covenant for virgins. Celebration ensued when the bride and groom exited with bloodstained (seal of a covenant) sheets. This established that the women had been faithful to her now-husband before their union (see Deuteronomy 22:13–17).

- Today's traditional vows were originally part of the Sarum rite in Catholic Christian worship. The vows were then translated into English as part of the Book of Common Prayer in the 1500s.[25]

- The tradition of wedding rings is thousands of years old. The circular shape of the ring symbolizes eternity, with no beginning and no ending.

Regardless of the specific traditions involved, all in all, the wedding day is supposed to be a celebration bringing both "joy and gladness" (Psalm 45:15 NRSV) for the couple and for the witnesses in attendance (see Revelation 19:7).

Weddings are much more than big, elaborate events on which we spend tons of money just so we can get stuck with a bill later. No, they are a public profession of our devotion and love for our future spouse, and they're a formal establishment of the marriage covenant.

Our Wedding Day

As seems to be the case for most couples, our wedding day flew by. From the rehearsal to the end, it was all a blur. Nonetheless, it was a joyous occasion that we will cherish forever. Things did not go entirely as planned, but Kenady continued to tell me (Damien) to enjoy the process and not be stressed out over the hiccups or minor details. We were so thankful to have family and friends come from near and far to celebrate our union. We literally felt God's presence the whole weekend, and He filled us with so much peace. Even some of our groomsmen noticed God's hand. One said, "Man, there's no drama in your wedding." This was intentional, because we had prayed for the wedding to be focused on the right things. We also give credit to the amazing group of people who helped us and served in any capacity needed.

We could go into greater detail, but that would be another book in itself. Instead, we've decided to share some key lessons we learned:

Create a timetable for the rehearsal and wedding. We believe this is instrumental to your success. Not that you are competing or trying to win a race, but a plan helps everybody get to where they need to be. The earlier you have these items listed out and provided to your wedding party, the better. Most of our groomsmen and bridesmaids were married and had kids. If you have a "no children" wedding, like we did, scheduling is especially crucial. You have to think about others, even on your special day/weekend. Sending out notifications and reminders really helped the process for us and gave the day-of coordinator peace and direction.

Bridesmaids and groomsmen are important. Who you have next to you on your special day is very important. We got complimented by the hotel staff on how civil and respectable our wedding party was. Listen, just because someone is family doesn't mean he or she is ready to hold this important position. Kenady and I thought carefully about every single person within our party. We did not try to keep things "even" between our respective family and friends as we filled spots. Nope! Instead, we looked at their character and how involved these men and women were in our lives. People questioned my choice not to have my brothers as best men, but I personally knew my older brother had a lot on his plate, with four kids and his own company, so it would not be wise to ask him to handle this task. With my twin brother, I recognized that he possessed other gifts and skills, and it would have been both unfair and unwise to place the responsibilities of the best man on his shoulders. Therefore, I chose Justin Hart, and it worked out perfectly.

Be flexible. As we mentioned already, not everything worked as we'd planned. I (Damien) loathe being late, and at 3 p.m. I learned that Kenady still hadn't taken her pictures—her dress wasn't even on yet. My groomsmen were encouraging me, but I didn't want to hear it. However, after some time and deep breaths, I decided to let it go and let God. We were thirty-five minutes late, but our wedding was spectacular. We had to shorten our pictures, and paid the DJ a bit more to stay longer, but it was all worth it in the end.

Have fun. Remember that the wedding is still supposed to be fun! After getting over myself, I (Damien) decided to enjoy the day. Why be grumpy at your own wedding? Pastor Marty, the officiate, made sure everybody, including us, laughed and had fun. For my part, I noticed Kenady shaking at the very beginning of the ceremony and whispered, "Bruh, why you shaking?"—which made her laugh. We shared jokes and danced at the reception. It's a choice to be intentional to soak it up, let go, laugh, and have fun. Among other things, marriage is supposed to be enjoyable, so why not start on your wedding day?

Remember Who matters most. Finally, the most important aspect of marriage: its reflection of the salvation that Jesus offers. All of the customs, symbols, and metaphors throughout the Bible all point to that one thing, salvation. The Bible tells us of a joyous occasion when Jesus (i.e., the Lamb of God, who takes away the sins of the world) as the groom and the church as the bride are joined at His second coming (Revelation 19:6–9). We also find Jesus' parable of the wedding feast, in Matthew 22:1–14, which depicts the extension of salvation as an invitation—God's invitation to the church, or those who have accepted His one and only Son.

We wanted so many people at our wedding. Nevertheless, some people just could not make it. You probably weren't there, either. But we want to invite you to another wedding, the main event, which will be better than any earthly wedding. All you have to do is accept Jesus Christ as your Lord and Savior and follow Him, turning from a life of sin to a life of righteousness. We will be there. Will you?

If you want to make that all-important decision today, please pray the prayer below and find a Bible-based church to get plugged into. You won't regret it. We are super-excited for you!

Salvation Prayer

Lord, I confess that I am a sinner and repent of my sins and surrender my life over to You. Jesus, I believe You died on a cross, rose from the dead, and now are sitting at the right hand of the Father, interceding for us. I ask the Holy Spirit to baptize me and fill me up with the fruit of the Spirit and the gifts of the Spirit. Bring like-minded people into my life and direct me to a Bible-believing church so I can study how to become a true disciple of You. Thank You, Lord Jesus. Amen.

Chapter 16:
You're Married Now—What's Next?

After the wedding craze and the honeymoon adventures end, you come back home to your new normal as husband and wife. For some, this may be a difficult transition, but we encourage you to give each other grace as you both adapt to this radical life change. Our experience was definitely supernatural! Don't get us wrong: we obviously had to get accustomed to sharing a space. But it wasn't as hard as people sometimes make it out to be, and we found it way more enjoyable than challenging. We truly believe that can be attributed to doing things God's way, by His grace. When you are submitted unto Him, there are blessings evermore. That's why we are so gung-ho on doing courtship and marriage His way!

Four Tips for Life After the Wedding

We want to speak life, and not death, into your marriage and offer tips to help you transition as smoothly as possible. Too often we hear, "Oh, just wait until you come out of your honeymoon period and off cloud 9." "It's not going to be that amazing all the time, so enjoy it while you can." How depressing and discouraging is *that*? We want to give you hope and get you excited to start your life as a newlywed.

You *get* to make the most out of your marriage! It doesn't have to be like everyone else's. We know of multiple couples who are still in their honeymoon phase years, or decades, after "I do." You have the choice to create a marriage that is filled with love, joy, and peace. Yes, there will be trials, disagreements, and many opportunities to die to yourself, but the challenges are no reason or excuse to give up and stop putting forth effort. You have the opportunity to tend your marriage like a garden and make it beautiful. Before we end this book, we want to provide you with four key tips we feel are important to help you through your transition into being husband and wife:

1. *Learn how to become one.* This doesn't come as second nature. After all, you have been your own, individual self for most of your life. It's not automatic or easy for two people to think and function as one. This means learning how to share just about everything, like space, time, resources, and decisions. This might be easier for those who have grown up with multiple siblings (possibly even a twin!), but it's still our sin nature to think selfishly. I know for me (Kenady), it was hard to share closet space. After we returned from our honeymoon, Damien moved into our space, where I had moved in a week before the wedding. Naturally, I had taken up most (possibly all) of the closet space, but I had to think about how that would make him feel when he moved in. So I had to get rid of a lot of clothes (which was definitely necessary since I didn't even wear half the clothes I owned). I also got creative and made use of the available space with racks, bins, and under-bed storage. I didn't want him to think he was spending the night in my spot. It was our space, and I wanted him to feel at home, too.

Becoming one also means you have to get important things in order. We joined bank accounts, got our insurance in order, and worked to update our beneficiaries. It's also important to get your rhythm and schedules together so you can function and operate successfully. For us, it was a priority to have dinner together each night, but we also made a habit of scheduling personal time each day. Because we see each other a lot and live under the same roof, we have to be intentional about allowing ourselves thirty minutes of individual alone time, as needed, to unwind from a busy day. This is never taken personally because we understand it can be necessary if we want to remain mentally, emotionally, physically, and spiritually available for each other. I didn't want to give Damien only what little was left of me after a long day, and vice versa. No, we want to refill and recharge so we can connect and be engaged with each other daily. Create plans and schedules that work best for both of you, to make becoming one easier and more enjoyable.

2. Learn how to communicate as one. To some extent, this is a continuation of the first tip. Because you are one but in two different bodies, it is so important to learn how to communicate and pass signals to each other so you function properly as one. Your spouse doesn't have superpowers and can't read your mind or know where you are automatically. It's common courtesy to keep your spouse informed. Are you going to be home a little later because you have to get gas and run an errand? That is something you need to let your spouse know so he or she doesn't think something happened to you. Remember, you aren't single anymore—you can't just come and go as you please.

It's also important to communicate to prevent misunderstandings and unnecessary conflicts. I remember when Damien and I were setting up our place after coming back from the honeymoon. I wanted Damien to help me take the microwave out of the box and put it on the shelf. He told me he would help after he finished cleaning out his suitcase in a few minutes since he was almost done. I got a little offended because he didn't stop what he was doing right away to help me. So I proceeded to struggle and do it myself, in pride and impatience. I also gave him the cold shoulder for about thirty minutes. Then I said to myself, "This is silly. I don't want to let the enemy come between us and get any satisfaction from this." I forgave him without communicating about it.

Then Damien brought it up at dinner. He told me, "I could see you were upset about me not helping you immediately with the microwave. I just wanted to let you know how I like to work. Growing up, we were raised to finish one task before jumping to different tasks. If we didn't complete the task, we would get punished and even spanked for it. I was going to help you right after I finished. You weren't in dire need for the microwave at that time. It wasn't me not wanting to help you." That acknowledgment and explanation was so comforting to me. It corrected a misunderstanding that almost had me thinking I was unloved or rejected.

It's crucial to communicate and work through conflict, and fast, so the enemy won't get between y'all. You will always have to continue to learn your spouse as you grow deeper into marriage, as you both grow individually and collectively, and as the seasons change. Communication will remain vital throughout your marriage.

3. Learn to out-serve one another. As a Christian, you should find this a no-brainer, but it is not often discussed or easily done. We are all called to serve others, and that's especially true within marriage. Damien and I have been intentional about this since the beginning of our marriage: we seek to serve each other instead of being served. The beauty about this is that when you are focusing on serving your spouse out of love, and your spouse is looking to serve you out of love, you both get served. Because we are practicing this servant heart, neither of us feels drained, used, or uncared for. Instead, we experience peace and joy.

One time after we got married, when I was under the weather, Damien stepped up and out-served for nearly the entire weekend. As soon as I felt better, it was my heart to out-serve him since he had been so selfless and did everything without complaining. We don't serve out of obligation, but out of opportunity. We get to be each other's spouse, and we get to show each other the love of Christ. Thus, we grow closer and more in love. Learn to be aware of what could be done or what needs to be done. If your spouse is cooking, take the initiative to set the table. If your spouse washed some clothes but has gotten behind on folding them, fold the clothes without being asked for your help. It's not about whose job it is, but about how you can help serve the other person, to let your spouse know you care enough to help share the load. Serving each other in this way will make for a much more pleasant marriage and home.

4. Learn how to encourage each other instead of criticizing. To be honest, this is the one with which we struggle most. More times than we would like to admit, we have criticized each other for not washing dishes a certain way or making the bed a certain way. As newlyweds coming together, it is hard to not have things done your way all of the time. You might want the clothes folded a certain way or put in a certain place, but your spouse folded the clothes a different way and put your clothes in the drawer instead of hung up in the closet. There is a temptation to criticize and say, "Why didn't you hang my stuff up? I don't want it folded." The better choice would be to say, "Thank you so much for folding my clothes. I really appreciate it." If you criticize your spouse after he or she has made a sweet gesture, you are discouraging similar gestures in the future. Yes, it's okay to communicate things, but do it with love and discernment about your words and timing.

Also, choose your battles. Surely there's more than one acceptable way to wash dishes or clean up the bathroom. Learn to give grace and to point out the good, not only the bad. You don't want to nag each other about details that don't really matter anyway, which will only result in mutual frustration and exhaustion. You'll have to give up certain things in marriage and learn how to work together, which sometimes means letting your spouse work the way he or she wants to.

In the Bible, the Love Chapter (1 Corinthians 13) says in part that love doesn't remember wrongs. The flip side of this is that love can remember "rights." So choose to remember the things your spouse has done right in order to encourage and build up him or her. Don't compare each other to other people's spouses, either, because that will cause you to be discontent and try to manipulate each other into being like someone else, who you are not meant to be. You might hear that someone's husband cooks her meals every Saturday and now feel resentful or envious because your husband doesn't cook at all. Perhaps your husband isn't gifted in the kitchen but does help you with the dishes after you cook every night. Appreciate the gift you have in each other and thank your spouse for what he or she does. Don't compare your grass for someone else's, because their grass might be fake. You never know what's really going on. Instead, tend to your own marriage and enjoy the blessings God has entrusted you to steward.

Discipled Couples, Disciple Couples!

This section is ultimately why we wrote the book. After receiving information, sometimes people keep it to themselves. We believe that as you read this book and begin applying its principles within your current relationship, no matter what stage you are in, you should pay it forward. By this, we mean you should pour into others as you have been poured into.

Before Jesus left the earth, He commanded His disciples to go and make disciples (Matthew 28:19). We have benefited tremendously by being discipled by couples, so we want to turn around and disciple other couples who are courting, or already married, to help teach them and hold them accountable. After all, discipleship must be an ongoing process, or it will eventually die off. We want godly courting, leading to godly marriages, to spread like wildfire. Too often, we have seen couples get married and disappear. But that's not going to be you!

There is beauty in discipling. It will help sharpen your marriage and continue to hold you accountable. Just think about a person or a couple who can benefit from the information you have learned and the experience you have acquired. Pray, and allow the Holy Spirit to highlight them.

As we close this book we want to give you a few more things to think about and share advice regarding discipling couples.

Be Present

For those who are married, we understand there is a time during which you need to establish your home. This period might be six months or one year, but regardless, we encourage you not to fall off the face of the earth, away from the courting couples in your circle of influence and/or your biblical community. There should be a point at which you are intentional to throw your hat back in the ring and tell people you are open to mentoring. Keep in mind that some couples are graced to have several couples at a time while others mentor only one couple a year. It might be wise to start off with just one in the beginning stages of your marriage and maybe grow to handling more down the road. But one is better than none!

Be Transparent

It's one thing to say you want to disciple a couple, and even meet up with the couple, but there is one important step you need to be willing to take: you must be willing to share openly about what you are going through or went through within your own relationship. Mentoring situations can too easily turn into one-way conversations where you are coaching and counseling the other couple but don't share your own struggles and frustrations. Two-way conversation creates a space where the other couple can connect with you as you reach into your personal experience to share practical, first-hand knowledge to help them avoid pitfalls. Our goal is to inform our couples with transparency and equip them with reliable biblical knowledge so they can be aware and not fall into traps that causes disunity in their relationships.

Be Teachable

Remember that this mentoring process is not just for those whom you are discipling. It's also for you, as the mentors. We learn a lot from others, even less-experienced couples, because we don't have all the answers. The couple you are discipling might be very good at communicating and how they handle disagreements, and if you don't go into the meetings humbly, you can miss some key advice. So our counsel here is simple: be humble and teachable. This will help keep you accountable and continue to grow you in your relationship as you help others.

Be in Community

Finally, we suggest that you not isolate yourselves from community. Yes, it's important to disciple couples, but what about you? Who is pouring into you? We encourage every couple to join a small group, perhaps one that's specifically for married couples. This is important so you have other couples holding you accountable as a married couple. We know that involvement in a small group might not be feasible for a season, but don't make busyness an excuse to avoid prioritizing community. We're all busy!

But what should you do if your church does not offer this kind of small group? Start your own. You can gather other married couples in your area, or even one other couple. We're sure you are not the only local couple wanting to get into community. Think about activities you enjoy. Do you like to work out, drink coffee, go to parks, dance, paint, or shoot short films? You can use social media or platforms like Meetup to organize activities and create your own community. You might decide to incorporate Bible study to bring additional spiritual enrichment to your group as well. Different people can help in various capacities so it's not always on you. There are plenty of possibilities, but you must be intentional. Remember to pray and ask God for ideas. Don't you think He would answer prayers that focus on unity and bringing people together to cultivate healthy relationships in your city? I'm sure He does!

We are still working through all of this ourselves. We don't have it all figured out, but we have been blessed to have great people around us, who have offered us valuable information and advice that we have passed along to you in this book.

Each of us is called to go higher and level up—that's what our King expects of us. As we do, we don't neglect the community and people around us. We are praying for you and also that you take this information and use it to help change your local church, which will in turn transform your city and, eventually, our world. And we are rooting for you as you become #CompletelyMarried! Wherever you are in the journey—single, dating (courting), engaged, or already married—we believe we are all family. If you are about to get married, we pray that you invite God into your relationship, to make your journey to the altar and beyond a special one, exactly as He intended.

About the Authors

Damien K. H. Nash, an award-winning Certified Growth Coach and author of #CompletelySingle, teams up with his wife, Kenady Nash, to write their first book together. Damien and Kenady were married in September 2019, but they began writing #CompletelyMarried when they first started courting, back in 2018. They believe their purpose is to help individuals become healthier—physically, emotionally, and spiritually—and in turn, to help them cultivate healthy relationships. Their YouTube channel, "Damien and Kenady," is used to deliver content that supports this passion. Damien and Kenady have had several speaking opportunities across the country, sharing the wisdom God has given them with whomever is willing to listen.

Acknowledgments

First and foremost, we would like to thank our Lord and Savior, Jesus Christ. Without God, we would never have had the inspiration or the wisdom to complete this book. Everything we do is because of God's grace and favor in our lives. God, we love serving You.

Secondly, we want to thank our families, the Nashes and the Pitts, especially our parents. Thank you for raising us in the faith and teaching us principles to live by, which have helped us develop our own personal relationships with God. Also, thanks to our siblings just for being there when we needed you. We love all of you.

To our many friends near and far, thank you for your continuous encouragement and support. We are blessed to have a great community around us who have believed in us from the beginning.

We would also like to thank our church family at Victory Church. Without the vision of our lead pastors, Dennis and Colleen Rouse, we would not have had a church building in which to meet each other! Thank you for giving us such a place to serve and attend, where we are fed the Word of God weekly, in an uncompromising way. Thanks also to all of the assistant ministers and staff for everything you do.

In particular, we would like to thank our accountability couple, Justin and Jasmine Hart. Your accountability and teaching have helped shape our relationship from the beginning. You two are a blessing to the kingdom of God, and your faithfulness to walk alongside couples is one of the many reasons we decided to write this book—just to let people know what level of accountability we have in our life. We are forever grateful, and we love you.

We can't forget Pastors Darius and Melba Dunson. You are our covering and a great example of what a godly marriage should look like. We are thankful for your friendship and your counsel throughout our engagement period and into our marriage. We are lifelong friends who love you and aren't going anywhere!

Last but definitely not least, we must thank Pastor Marty Barrett. Your counseling sessions were straight to the point and creative. Your love and charity throughout our relationship kept us focused on getting to the altar despite our faults and failures. Thank you for stepping in for our dad, who's dancing with the Lord. You made our wedding enjoyable and unforgettable. We love you.

#CompletelySingle:

Learning How to Become the Right One
Before Meeting the Right One

Single or Married, this is a winner!

I am amazed at the clarity and ingenuity that Damien has displayed in this book. He has captured deep insights into the struggle that various men and women go through as they seek to understand their destiny in relationship and marriage. —Amazon review

Know anyone who is single? Or are you single? I mean, are you completely single? No matter whether you are engaged, courting (dating), or single looking to mingle, it is important to answer this question honestly and prayerfully. God desires us to be whole, especially before we enter into a serious relationship. One of the reasons why relationships are short-lived—or long and painful—is because we as a society don't seek to enter the relationship completely single.

#CompletelySingle shows how Adam was completely single while in a relationship with God before he even knew he needed Eve. Once we seek after singleness wholeheartedly, our relationships will begin to blossom as God intended!

This book will help you acknowledge the areas that are causing you not to be single. It will help you accept God's plan for your singleness and apply biblical principles to align your behavior with His plan. Married couples can also benefit from this book: by identifying the boundaries that might have been crossed before and after you said, "I do!" you can get to the root of contention in your marriage. Friends, let's get back to the basics by looking at the biblical principles found in the very first relationship—as we seek to become #CompletelySingle.

Don't forget to Follow Damien and Kenady on Instagram @DamienandKenady.

And head over to DamienandKenady.com for more books and merchandise!

References:
Works Cited

1. Merriam-Webster, "dysentery (noun)." https://www.merriam-webster.com/dictionary/dysentery.

2. Merriam-Webster, "accountability (noun)." https://www.merriam-webster.com/dictionary/accountability.

3. Smith, Sylvia. "Levels of Communication in Marriage." Marriage.com. https://www.marriage.com/advice/communication/levels-of-communication-in-marriage.

4. Chapman, Gary. *The Five Love Languages*. Northfield Publishing, 2010.

5. Barna, George. The Power of Vision: Discover and Apply God's Plan for Your Life and Ministry. Baker Books, 2009.

6. Merriam-Webster, "azimuth (noun)." https://www.merriam-webster.com/dictionary/azimuth.

7. Stoltzfus, Tony. Coaching Questions: *A Coach's Guide to Powerful Asking Skills*. BookSurge, 2008.

8. Nash, Damien. *#CompletelySingle*. TNG Publishings, 2015.

9. Nash, *#CompletelySingle*.

10. Steverman, Ben. "The Latest Thing Millennials Are Being Blamed for Killing? Divorce." Time. September 25, 2018. https://time.com/5405757/millennials-us-divorce-rate-decline.

11. Laumann, E. O., D. B. Glasser, R. C. S. Neves, and E. D. Moreira, Jr. "A Population-Based Survey of Sexual Activity, Sexual Problems and Associated Help-Seeking Behavior Patterns in Mature Adults in the United States of America." International Journal of Impotence Research 21 (2009), p. 171–178. In Nature.com. February 26, 2009. https://www.nature.com/articles/ijir20097.

12. Laumann et al., "A Population-Based Survey," 2009.

13. Zilbergeld, Bernie. *The New Male Sexuality: The Truth About Men, Sex, and Pleasure*. Bantam, 1993.

14. Strong, Bryan, and Theodore F. Cohen. *The Marriage and Family Experience: Intimate Relationships in a Changing Society*. 13th ed. Cengage Learning, 2016.

15. Strong and Cohen, *The Marriage and Family Experience*.

References:
Works Cited

16. Nierenberg, Cari. "Am I Having a Boy or Girl?—Ultrasound and Sex Prediction." Live Science. December 21, 2017. https://www.livescience.com/45582-boy-or-girl.html.

17. Mr. prince. "A Good Woman Dr Myles Monroe Speaks on How to Fix Issues with Male Female Relationship." May 9, 2018. https://www.youtube.com/watch?v=TLiVmQlAmzo.

18. Guzik, David. "Exodus 19 —The Nation of Israel Comes to Mount Sinai." Enduring Word. 2018. https://enduringword.com/bible-commentary/exodus-19.

19. Merriam-Webster, "consecrate (adjective)." https://www.merriam-webster.com/dictionary/consecrate.

20. McIntyre, Todd. "Real Men Love." Victory Church. https://victoryatl.com/messages-item/realmenlove.

21. "Strong's G3860—paradidomi." Blue Letter Bible. https://www.blueletterbible.org/lang/lexicon/lexicon.cfm?page=3&strongs=g3860&t=kjv#lexResults.

22. Merriam-Webster, "tarry (verb)." https://www.merriam-webster.com/dictionary/tarry.

23. Cady, Nick. "The Impact on Kids of Dad's Faith and Church Attendance." Longmont Pastor. June 20, 2016. https://nickcady.org/2016/06/20/the-impact-on-kids-of-dads-faith-and-church-attendance.

24. Merriam-Webster, "steadfast (adjective)." https://www.merriam-webster.com/dictionary/steadfast.

25. "History of Traditional Wedding Vows." Pynes House. July 24, 2015. https://www.pyneshouse.co.uk/history-of-traditional-wedding-vows.

References:
Works Consulted

Abundant Life Christian Fellowship. "Dating—The Talk." YouTube video. April 30, 2017. https://www.youtube.com/watch?v=roAHDzIy4vI.

Abundant Life Christian Fellowship. "Healing Broken Relationships—Part 2." YouTube video. June 25, 2018. https://youtu.be/aFG9iSnq8rg.

Bolz, Shawn. *Translating God: Hearing God's Voice for Yourself and the World Around You*. iCreate Productions, 2015.

"Exodus 19." Coffman's Commentaries on the Bible. In StudyLight.org. https://www.studylight.org/commentaries/bcc/exodus-19.html.

Groeschel, Craig, and Amy Groeschel. *From This Day Forward: Five Commitments to Fail-Proof Your Marriage*. Curriculum kit. Zondervan, 2014.

Laan, Ray Vander. "To Be a Talmid." That the World May Know. https://www.thattheworldmayknow.com/to-be-a-talmid.

TED-Ed. "The History of Marriage—Alex Gendler." YouTube video. February 13, 2014. https://youtu.be/ZZZ6QB5TSfk.

Zodhiates, Spiro, ed. *The Hebrew–Greek Key Word Study Bible: King James Version*. 2nd revised ed. 1984. AMG International, 2008.

NOTES

#COMPLETELYMARRIED

NOTES

DAMIEN K. H. NASH AND KENADY NASH

#COMPLETELYMARRIED

NOTES